MPLE SO

est Tunes to Strum & Sing on Ukulele

ISBN 978-1-4950-5972-8

Visit Hal Leonard Online at
www.halleonard.com

Contact Us:
Hal Leonard
7777 West Bluemound Road
Milwaukee, WI 53213
Email: info@halleonard.com

In Europe contact:
Hal Leonard Europe Limited
42 Wigmore Street
Marylebone, London, W1U 2RN
Email: info@halleonardeurope.com

In Australia contact:
Hal Leonard Australia Pty. Ltd.
4 Lentara Court
Cheltenham, Victoria, 3192 Australia
Email: info@halleonard.com.au

CONTENTS

All Along the Watchtower

Words and Music by Bob Dylan

1. There must be some kind of way out-ta here,
2., 4. *See additional lyrics*
3. *Instrumental solo*

said the jok - er to the thief. There's too much con - fu - sion.

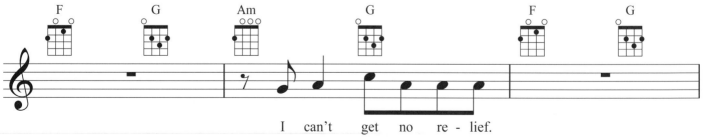

I can't get no re - lief.

Additional Lyrics

2. No reason to get excited, the thief, he kindly spoke.
   There are many here among us who feel that life is but a joke.
   But you and I, we've been through that, and this is not our fate.
   So let us not talk falsely now; the hour's gettin' late.

4. Well, all along the watchtower, princes kept the view
   While all the women came and went, barefoot servants too.
   Outside in the cold distance, a wild cat did growl.
   Two riders were approachin', and the wind began to howl.

Aloha Oe

Words and Music by Queen Liliuokalani

vale. _____ Fare - well to

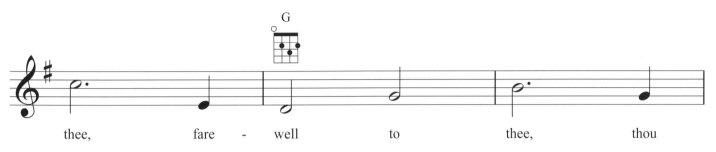

thee, fare - well to thee, thou

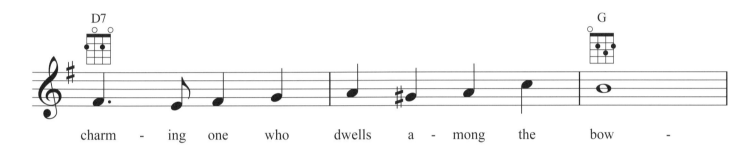

charm - ing one who dwells a - mong the bow -

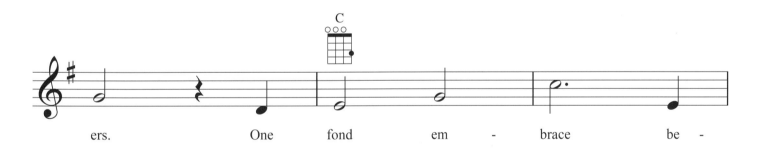

ers. One fond em - brace be -

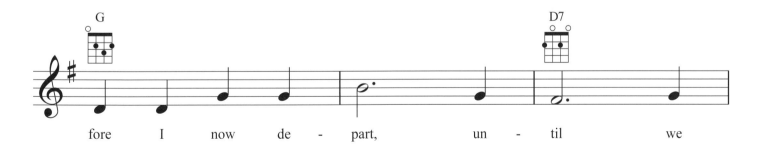

fore I now de - part, un - til we

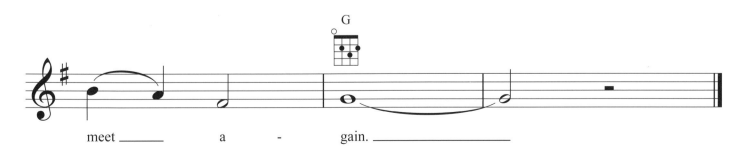

meet _____ a - gain. _____

The Beat Goes On

Words and Music by Sonny Bono

The beat goes on, _____ the beat goes on. _____

_____ Drums keep pound - ing rhy - thm to the

brain. La da da da di. La da da

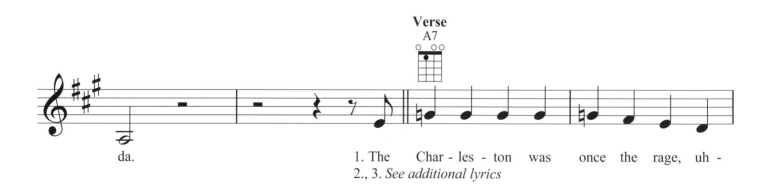

da. 1. The Char - les - ton was once the rage, uh -
2., 3. *See additional lyrics*

huh.   His - to - ry has turned a page, uh -

huh.   The min - i - skirt's the cur - rent thing, uh -

huh.   Teen - y bop - per is our

Last time, D.S. and fade

new - born king, uh - huh.   And the beat goes on, ___

Additional Lyrics

2. The grocery store's a supermart, uh-huh.
 Little girls still break their hearts, uh-huh.
 And men still keep on marching off to war.
 Electrically they keep a baseball score.

3. Grandmas sit in chairs and reminisce.
 Boys keep chasing girls to get a kiss.
 The cars keep going faster all the time.
 Bum still cries, "Hey, buddy, have you got a dime?"

Burning House

Words and Music by Jeff Bhasker, Tyler Sam Johnson and Camaron Ochs

First note

Moderately fast

1. I had a dream a - bout a burn - in' house. _____
(2.) see you at a par - ty and you look the same. _____

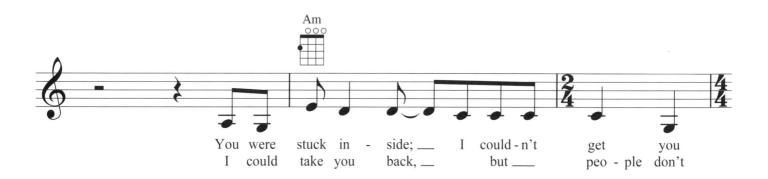

You were stuck in - side; _____ I could - n't get you
I could take you back, _____ but _____ peo - ple don't

out. _____
ev - er change. _____

I laid be - side _____ you and
Wish that we _____ could go

N.C.

pulled you close. _____
back in time. _____

And the
I'd _____

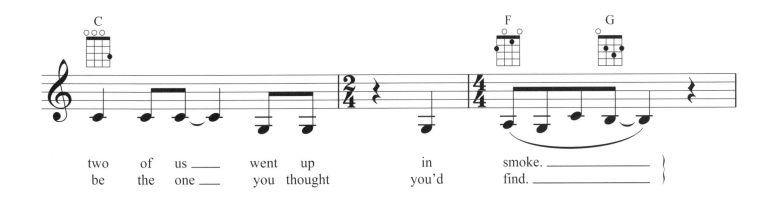

two of us ____ went up   in   smoke. _____
be the one ____ you thought   you'd   find. _____

Pre-Chorus

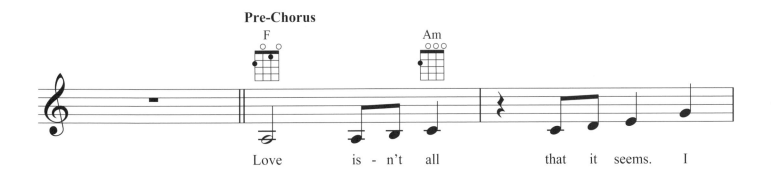

Love   is - n't all   that   it   seems.   I

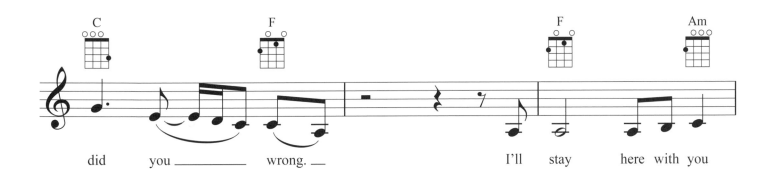

did   you _____ wrong. ____   I'll   stay   here with you

un - til this dream   is ____ gone.   I've been

𝄋 Chorus

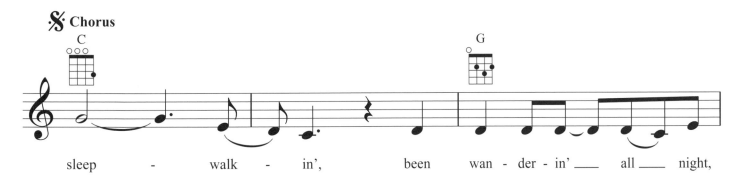

sleep - walk - in',   been wan - der - in' ____ all ____ night,

tryin' to take ___ what's lost ___ and broke ___ and make __ it right.

I've been sleep - walk - in'

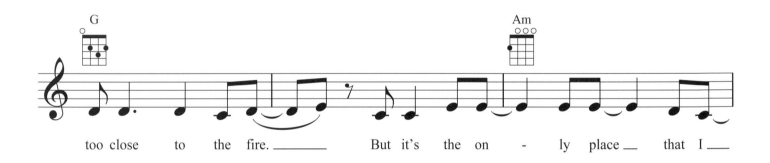

too close to the fire. _____ But it's the on - ly place ___ that I ___

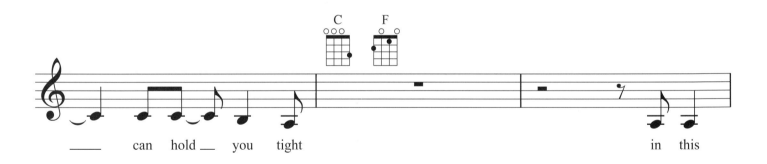

___ can hold ___ you tight in this

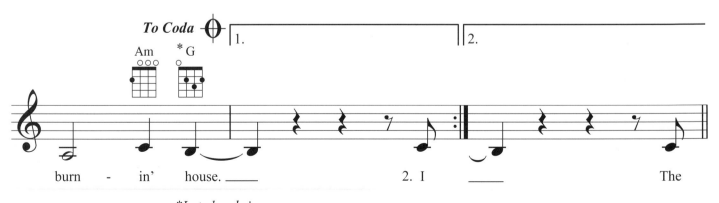

burn - in' house. _____ 2. I ___ The

Let chord ring.

Bridge

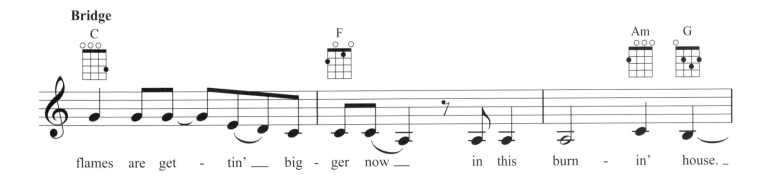

flames are get - tin' __ big - ger now __ in this burn - in' house. __

__ I can hold __ on to __ you some - how in this

burn - in' house. ___ Oh, __ and I don't wan - na wake __

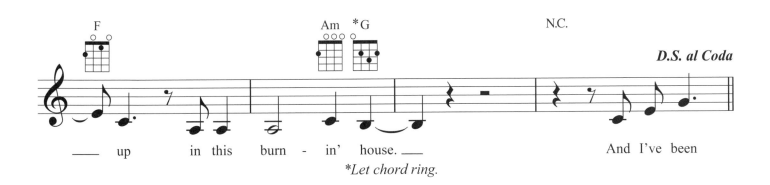

__ up in this burn - in' house. __ And I've been

Let chord ring.

Coda

Outro

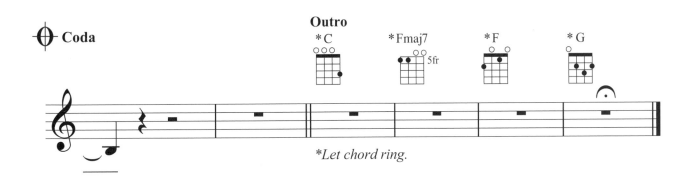

Let chord ring.

Bye Bye Love

Words and Music by Felice Bryant and Boudleaux Bryant

1. There goes my ba - by _____ with some - one new; _____
(2.) ro - mance, _ I'm through with love. _____

_____ she sure looks hap - py; _____ I sure am blue. _____
_____ I'm through with count - ing _____ the stars a - bove; _____

_____ She was my ba - by _____ till he stepped in; _____
_____ and here's the rea - son _____ that I'm so free: _____

_____ good-bye to ro - mance _____ that might have been. _____
_____ my lov - in' ba - by _____ is through with me. _____

Chorus

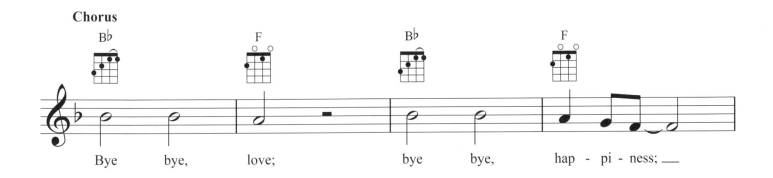

Bye bye, love; bye bye, hap - pi - ness; __

hel - lo, lone - li - ness; __ I think I'm gon - na cry. ____

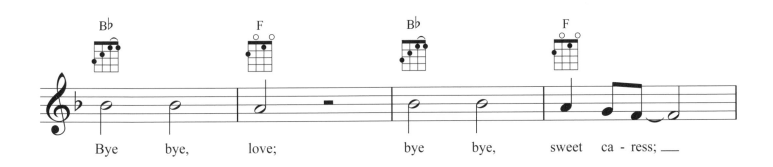

Bye bye, love; bye bye, sweet ca - ress; __

hel - lo, emp - ti - ness; __ I feel like I could die, ____ bye

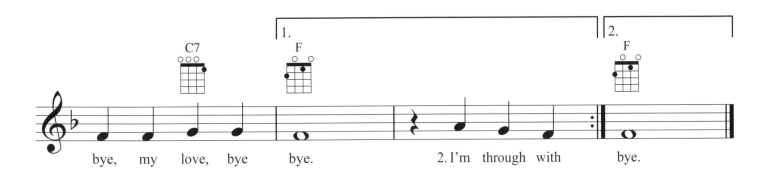

bye, my love, bye bye. 2. I'm through with bye.

Can't Help Falling in Love

from the Paramount Picture BLUE HAWAII

Words and Music by George David Weiss, Hugo Peretti and Luigi Creatore

Born on the Bayou

Words and Music by John Fogerty

First note

Verse
Moderately

G7

1. When I was just ___ a lit - tle boy,

stand - in' to my dad - dy's knee, ___ my

pa - pa said, "Son, don't let ___ the man get you and do ___

___ what he done to me. 'Cause he'll get you,

'cause he'll get you now, now."

𝄋 Verse

G7

2. I can re - mem - ber the Fourth ___ of Ju - ly, ___
3. Wish I was back ___ on the bay - ou,

run - nin' through the back - wood bare. ___ And
roll - in' with some Ca - jun queen. ___

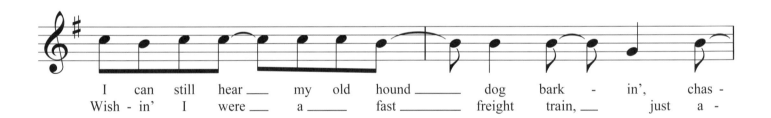

I can still hear ___ my old hound ___ dog bark - in', chas -
Wish - in' I were ___ a ___ fast ___ freight train, ___ just a -

To Coda ⊕

F   C

- in' down a hoo - doo there, ___ chas -
choo - glin' on ___ down to New ___

G7   F   C

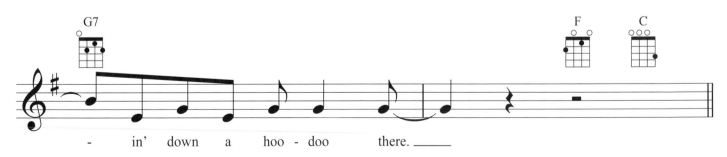

- in' down a hoo - doo there. ___

Born ___ on the bay - ou,

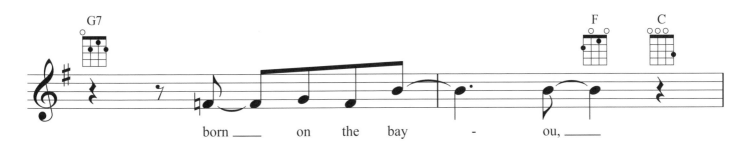

born ___ on the bay - ou, ___

born ___ on the bay - ou.

D.S. al Coda

⊕ **Coda**

Outro-Chorus

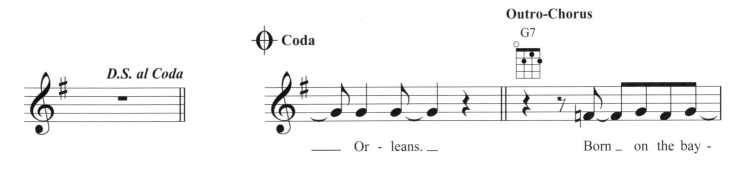

___ Or - leans. ___   Born ___ on the bay -

- ou,   born ___ on the bay - ou, ___

born ___ on the bay - ou.

Cheerleader

Words and Music by Omar Pasley, Mark Bradford, Clifton Dillon, Sly Dunbar and Ryan Dillon

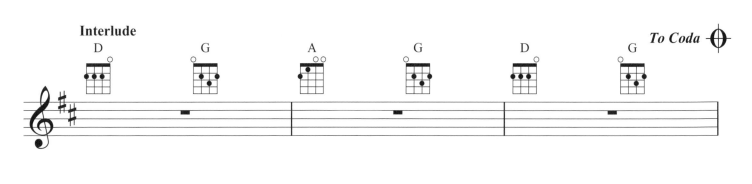

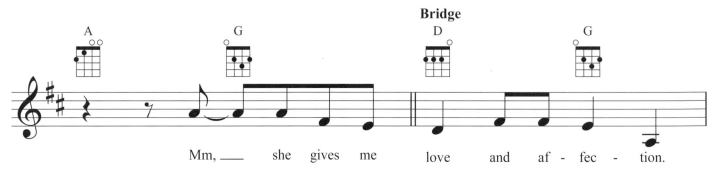

Mm, ___ she gives me love and af - fec - tion.

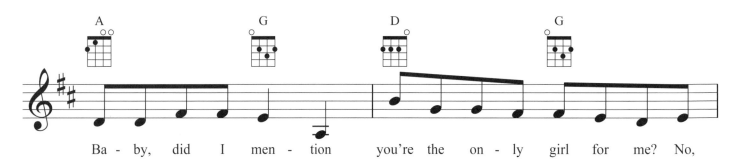

Ba - by, did I men - tion you're the on - ly girl for me? No,

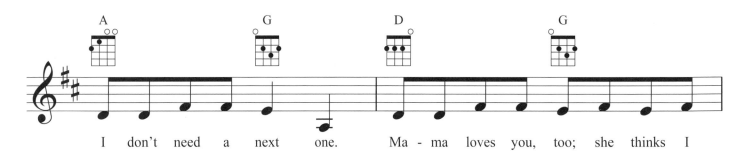

I don't need a next one. Ma - ma loves you, too; she thinks I

made the right se - lec - tion. Now all that's left to do is just for

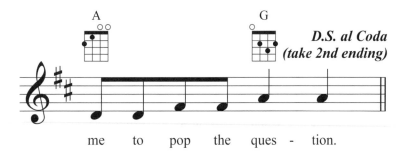

me to pop the ques - tion.

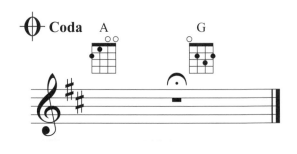

Copperhead Road

Words and Music by Steve Earle

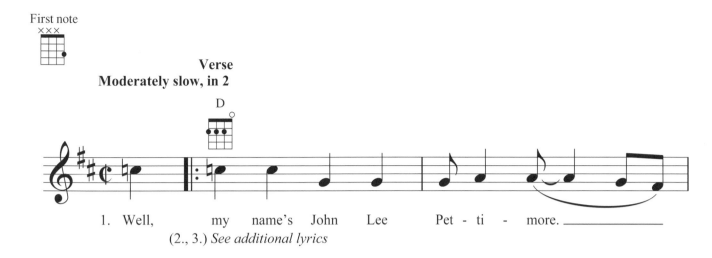

Verse
Moderately slow, in 2

1. Well,   my name's John Lee Pet - ti - more. _____
(2., 3.) *See additional lyrics*

Same as my dad - dy and his

dad - dy be - fore. _____   You

hard - ly ev - er saw Grand - dad - dy down here. _____

He on - ly come to town a - bout twice _ a year. _

He'd buy a hun - dred pounds of yeast and some

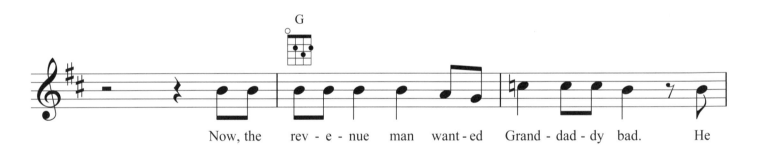

cop - per line.

Ev - 'ry - bod - y knew that he made moon - shine.

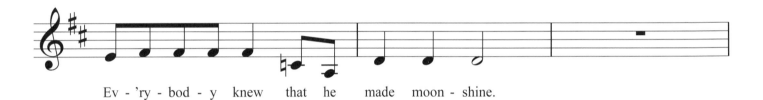

G

Now, the rev - e - nue man want - ed Grand - dad - dy bad. He

D   G

head - ed up a hol - ler with ev - 'ry - thing he had. __ Be - fore my time, __ but I've __

D

__ been told __ he nev - er come back from Cop - per - head Road. _____

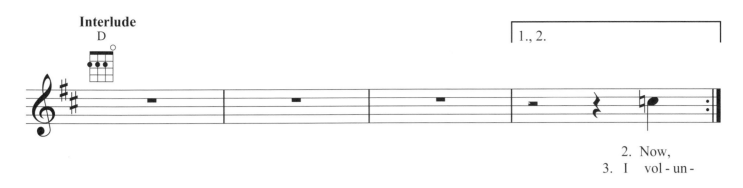

Interlude

1., 2.

2. Now,
3. I vol-un-

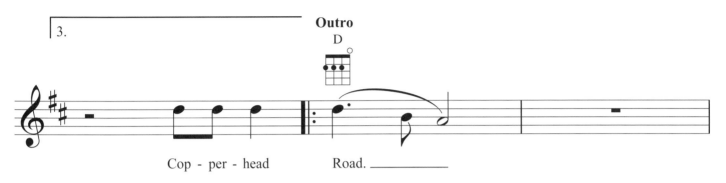

3.

Outro

Cop - per - head   Road. _____

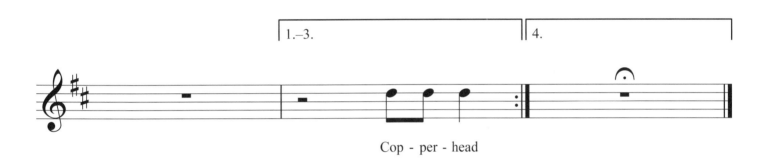

1.–3.

4.

Cop - per - head

Additional Lyrics

2. Now, Daddy ran the whiskey in a big-block Dodge.
Bought it at an auction at the Mason's Lodge.
"Johnson County Sheriff" painted on the side.
Just shot a coat of primer, then he looked inside.
Well, him and my uncle tore that engine down.
I still remember that rumblin' sound.
Then the sheriff came around in the middle of the night.
I heard Mama cryin'; knew somethin' wasn't right.
He was headed down to Knoxville with the weekly load.
You could smell the whiskey burnin' down Copperhead Road.

3. I volunteered for the Army on my birthday.
They draft the white trash first 'round here anyway.
I done two tours of duty in Vietnam.
I came home with a brand-new plan.
I'd take the seed from Colombia and Mexico.
I'd just plant it up a holler down Copperhead Road.
Now the DEA's got a chopper in the air.
I wake up screamin' like I'm back over there.
I learned a thing or two from Charlie, don't you know.
You better stay away from Copperhead Road.

Coconut

Words and Music by Harry Nilsson

First note

Verse
Moderately

1. Broth-er bought a co-co-nut, he bought it for the dime. His sis-ter

had an-oth-er one, she paid it for the lime. ___ She put the

Chorus

lime in the co-co-nut, she drank 'em both ___ up. She put the
lime in the co-co-nut, you drank 'em both ___ up, put the

lime in the co-co-nut, she drank 'em both ___ up. She put the
lime in the co-co-nut, you drank 'em both ___ up, put the

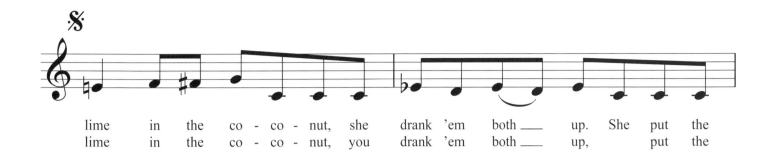

lime   in   the   co - co - nut,   she   drank 'em both ___ up. She   put   the
lime   in   the   co - co - nut,   you   drank 'em both ___ up,   put   the

lime   in   the   co - co - nut,   she   called the   doc - tor, woke him up   and said,
lime   in   the   co - co - nut,   you   called your doc - tor, woke him up   and said,

Bridge

"Doc - tor,   ain't there   noth - in' I   can   take,   I   said,   Doc -

- tor,   to   re - lieve this bel - ly ache? I   said,

To Coda 1 ⊕

Doc - tor,   ain't there   noth - in' I   can   take,   I   said,

Doc - tor, to re - lieve this bel - ly ache?" Now

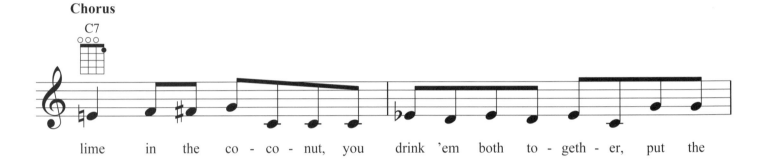

let me get this straight. 2. You put the lieve this bel - ly ache?" You put the

Chorus

C7

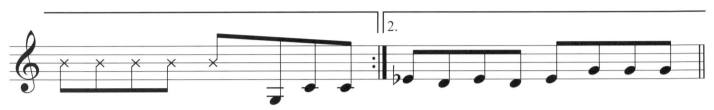

lime in the co - co - nut, you drink 'em both to - geth - er, put the

lime in the co - co - nut, then ____ you feel bet - ter. Put the

lime in the co - co - nut, drink 'em both ____ up, put the

lime in the co - co - nut and call me in the morn - ing.

Interlude

Woo, _____ woo, ___ oo, oo, _____ oo, _____ oo. _____

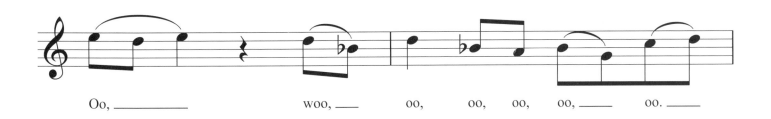

Oo, _____ woo, ___ oo, oo, oo, oo, _____ oo.

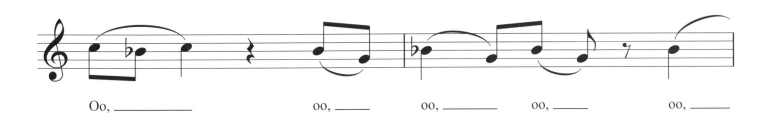

Oo, _____ oo, ___ oo, _____ oo, ___ oo, _____

_____ oo, _____ oo, _____ oo, _____ oo, _____ oo. _____

Verse

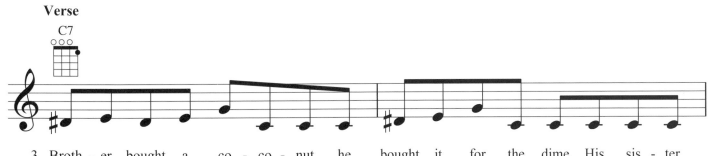

3. Broth - er bought a co - co - nut, he bought it for the dime. His sis - ter

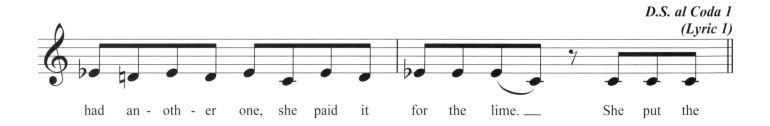

had an - oth - er one, she paid it for the lime. ___ She put the

Coda 1

Doc - tor, now let me get this straight." 4. You put the

Chorus

C7

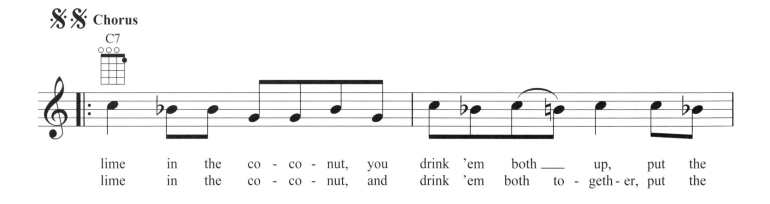

lime in the co - co - nut, you drink 'em both ___ up, put the
lime in the co - co - nut, and drink 'em both to - geth - er, put the

lime in the co - co - nut, you drink 'em both ___ up, the
lime in the co - co - nut, then you feel bet - ter. Put the

To Coda 2

lime in the co - co - nut, you drink 'em both ___ up, put the
lime in the co - co - nut, drink 'em both ___ { down, up, } put the

lime   in   the   co - co - nut,   you're   such   a   sil - ly   wom - an.   Put   a
lime   in   the   co - co - nut,   and

Bridge

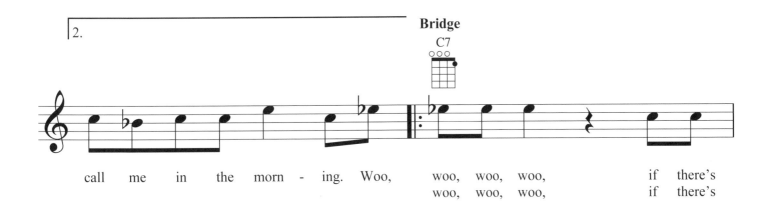

call   me   in   the   morn - ing.   Woo,   woo, woo, woo,   if   there's
                                     woo, woo, woo,   if   there's

noth - ing   you   can   take,   I   said,   woo, woo, woo, woo,   to   re -
noth - ing   I   can   take."   I   say,   woo, _____ woo,   to   re -

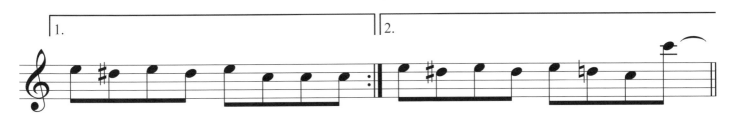

lieve   your   bel - ly   ache.   You   say,   "Well,   lieve   your   bel - ly   ache.   You   say,   "Yeah, __

____   if   there's   noth - ing   I   can   take."   I   say,   wow, __
____   da,   if   there's   noth - ing   I   can   take.   I   say,   dat, __
____   da,   if   there's   noth - ing   I   can   take.   I   say,   dat, __

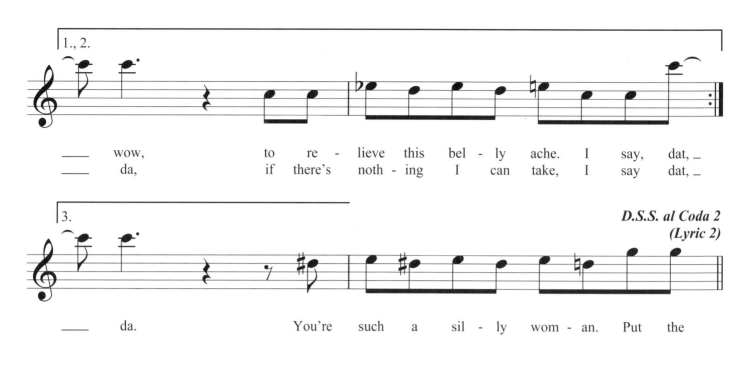

_____ wow, to re - lieve this bel - ly ache. I say, dat, _____
_____ da, if there's noth - ing I can take, I say dat, _____

D.S.S. al Coda 2
(Lyric 2)

_____ da. You're such a sil - ly wom - an. Put the

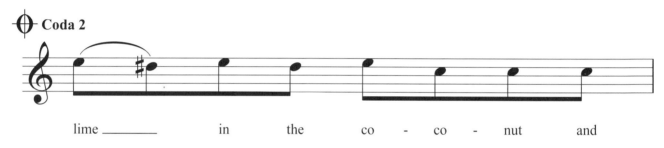

Coda 2

lime _____ in the co - co - nut and

Outro
C7

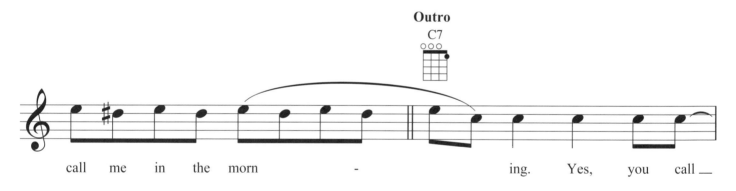

call me in the morn - ing. Yes, you call _____

_____ me in the morn - ing, when you call me in the morn - ing, I'll tell _____

Repeat and fade

_____ you what to do. If you call me in the morn - ing, I'll tell _____

Day-O
(The Banana Boat Song)

Words and Music by Irving Burgie and William Attaway

First note

Intro
Freely

N.C.

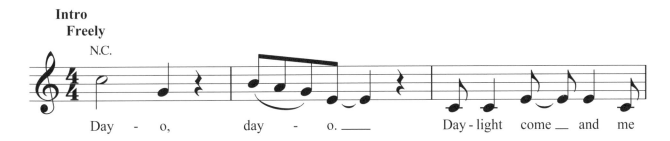

Day - o, day - o. ___ Day - light come ___ and me

wan' go home. ___ Day, me say day, me say day, me say day, me say day, me say

day - o. Day - light come ___ and me wan' go home. ___

Verse
Moderate Calypso

C

1. Work all night ___ on a drink of rum. ___ Day-light come ___ and me

G7   C

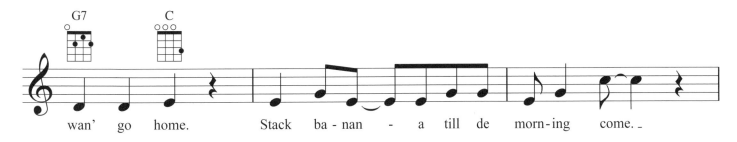

wan' go home. Stack ba - nan - a till de morn - ing come. ___

34

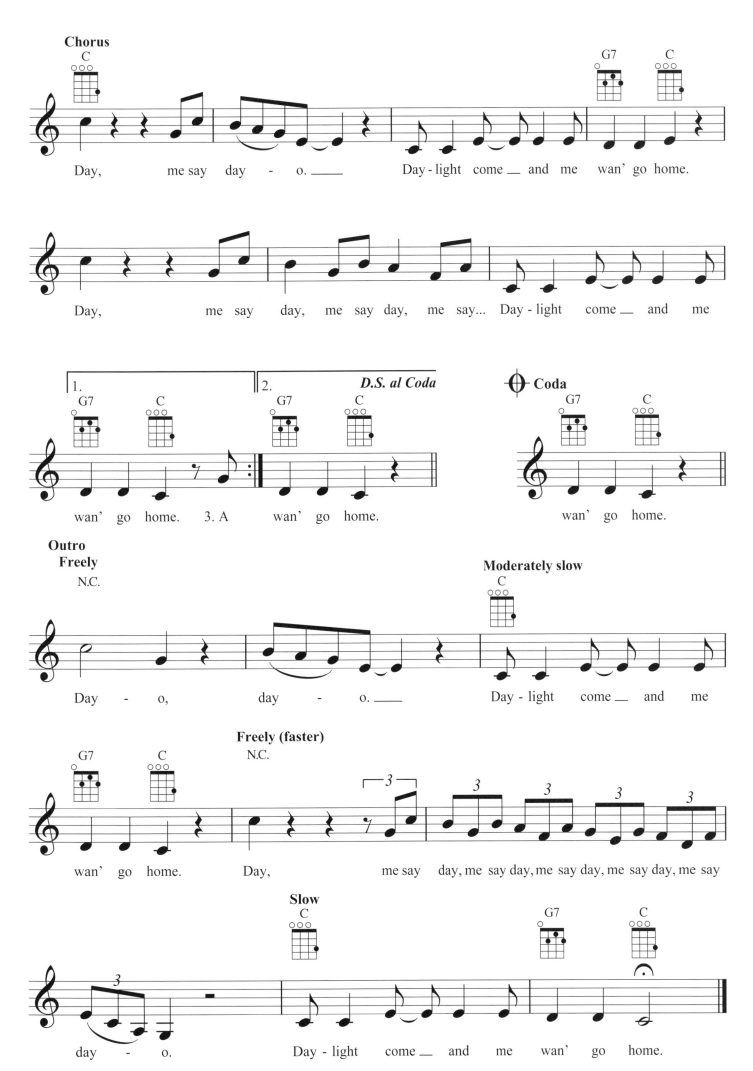

Deep in the Heart of Texas

Words by June Hershey
Music by Don Swander

First note

Verse
Moderately bright, in 2

1. The stars at night are big and
(2.) coy - otes wail a - long the

bright, deep in the heart of
trail, deep in the heart of

Tex - as. The prai - rie
Tex - as. The rab - bits

sky is wide and high,
rush a - round the brush,

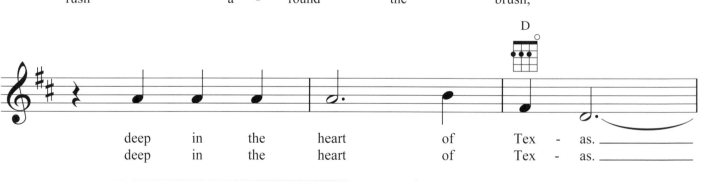

deep in the heart of Tex - as.
deep in the heart of Tex - as.

The sage in bloom is
The cow - boys cry, "Ki -

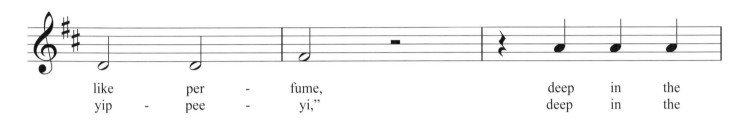

like per - fume,
yip - pee - yi,"
deep in the
deep in the

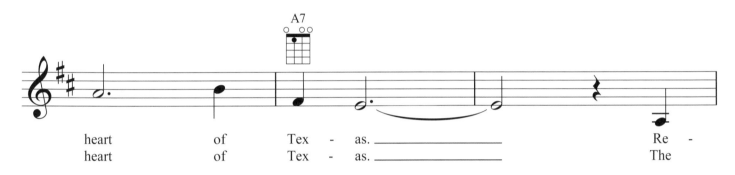

A7

heart of Tex - as. _____ Re -
heart of Tex - as. _____ The

minds me of the one I
do - gies bawl, and bawl and

love, deep in the heart of
bawl, deep in the heart of

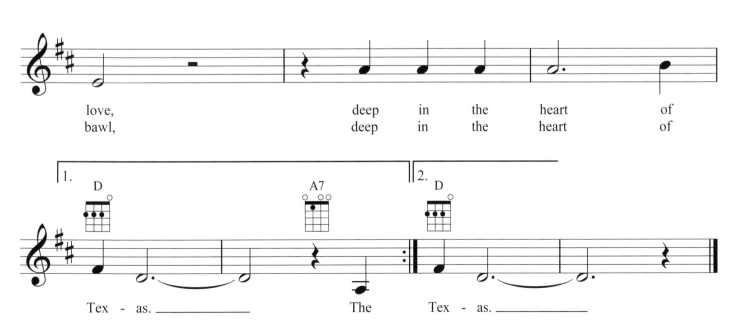

1.
D

A7

2.
D

Tex - as. _____ The
Tex - as. _____

Down by the Riverside

African-American Spiritual

Down on the Corner

Words and Music by John Fogerty

First note

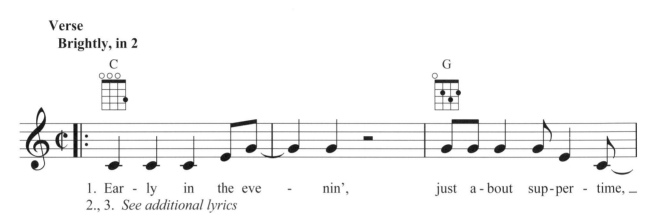

Verse
Brightly, in 2

1. Ear - ly in the eve - nin', just a - bout sup-per - time, __
2., 3. *See additional lyrics*

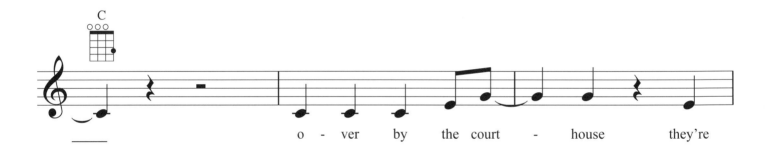

__ o - ver by the court - house they're

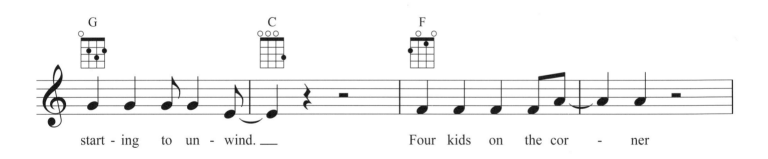

start - ing to un - wind. __ Four kids on the cor - ner

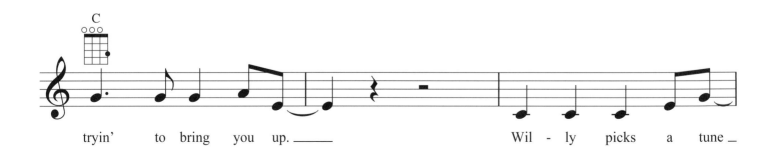

tryin' to bring you up. __ Wil - ly picks a tune __

_____ out and he blows it on the harp. _____

Chorus

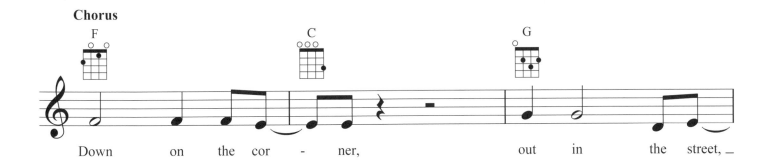

Down on the cor - ner, out in the street, __

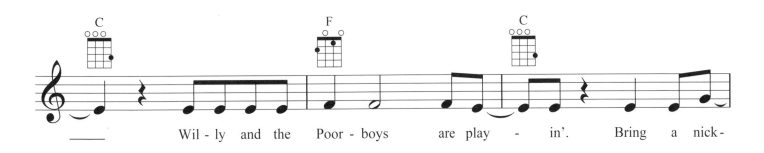

_____ Wil - ly and the Poor - boys are play - in'. Bring a nick-

1., 2.   3.

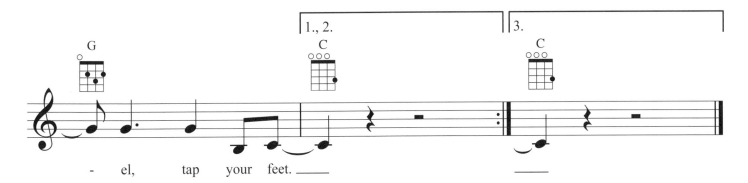

- el, tap your feet. _____   _____

Additional Lyrics

2. Rooster hits the washboard and people just gotta smile.
Blinky thumps the gut bass and solos for a while.
Poorboy twangs the rhythm out on his kalamazoo.
Willy goes into a dance and doubles on kazoo.

3. You don't need a penny just to hang around,
But if you've got a nickel, won't you lay your money down?
Over on the corner there's a happy noise.
People come from all around to watch the magic boy.

Dream Baby
(How Long Must I Dream)

Words and Music by Cindy Walker

Verse
Moderately, in 2

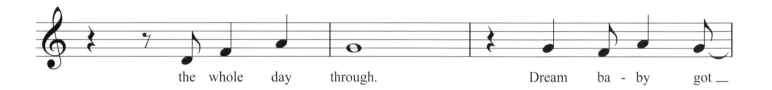

Dream ba - by got _____ me dream - in' sweet dreams

the whole day through. Dream ba - by got ___

___ me dream - in' sweet dreams night - time, too.

I love you and ___ I'm dream - in' of you, that won't

do. _____ Dream ba - by, make ____ me stop my dream - in';

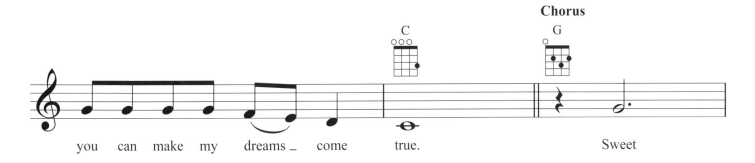

you can make my dreams _ come true.   Sweet

Chorus

dream   ba - by.   Sweet

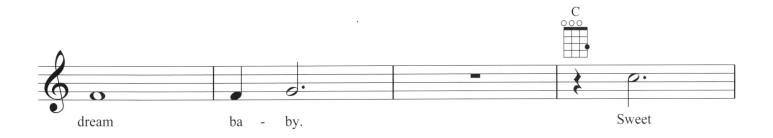

dream   ba - by.   Sweet

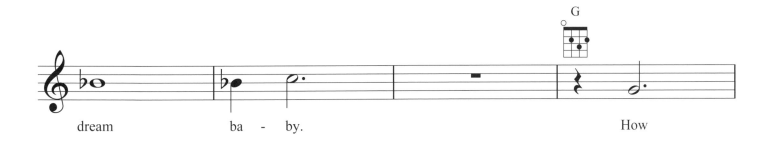

dream   ba - by.   How

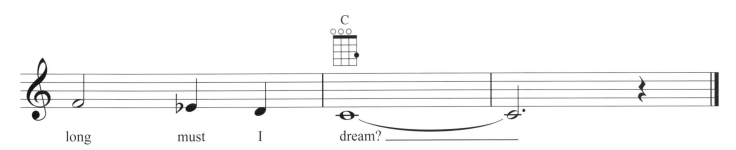

long   must   I   dream? _____

Eensy, Weensy Spider

Traditional

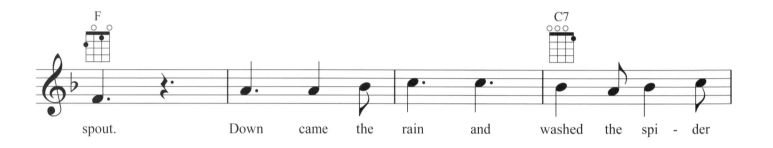

Een - sy, ween - sy spi - der went up the wa - ter -

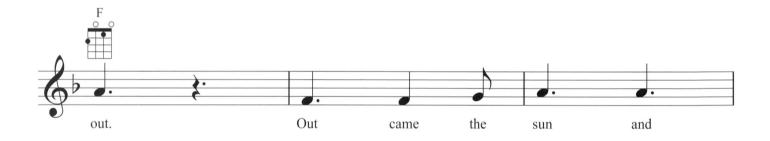

spout. Down came the rain and washed the spi - der

out. Out came the sun and

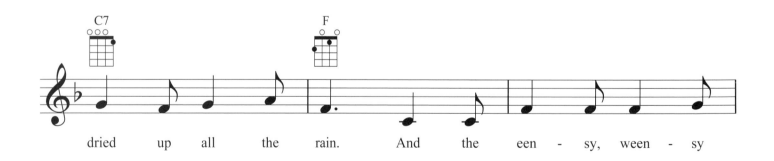

dried up all the rain. And the een - sy, ween - sy

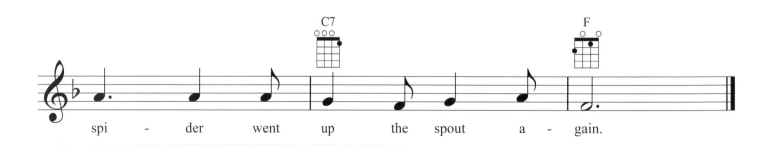

spi - der went up the spout a - gain.

Don't Worry, Be Happy

Words and Music by Bobby McFerrin

Verse
Moderate Reggae

1. Here's a lit - tle song I wrote. __ You

2., 3. *See additional lyrics*

might want to sing it note __ for note. __ Don't wor - ry,

be hap - py.

In ev - 'ry life we have __ some trou - ble,

but when you wor - ry you make __ it dou - ble. Don't

Additional Lyrics

2. Ain't got no place to lay your head.
   Somebody came and took your bed.
   Don't worry, be happy.
   The landlord say your rent is late,
   He may have to litigate.
   Don't worry, be happy.
   (Spoken:) Look at me— I'm happy.

3. Ain't got no cash, ain't got no style.
   Ain't got no gal to make you smile.
   Don't worry, be happy.
   'Cause when you worry your face will frown,
   And that will bring ev'rybody down.
   Don't worry, be happy.
   Don't worry, be happy now.

Fire on the Mountain

Words by Robert Hunter
Music by Mickey Hart

drowned in your laugh - ter and
But you're here a - lone; there's no
You gave all you had; why you

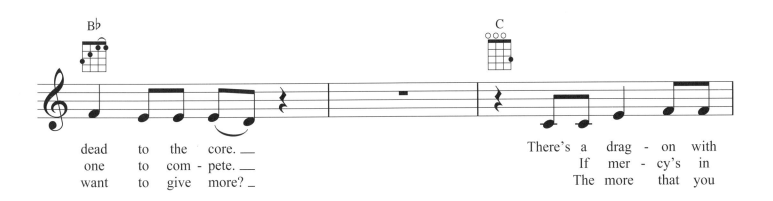

dead to the core. ___
one to com - pete. ___ There's a drag - on with
want to give more? ___ If mer - cy's in
The more that you

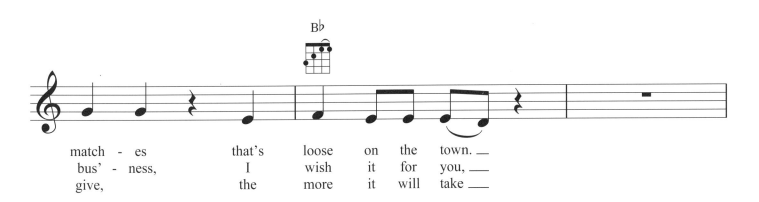

match - es that's loose on the town. ___
bus' - ness, I wish it for you, ___
give, the more it will take ___

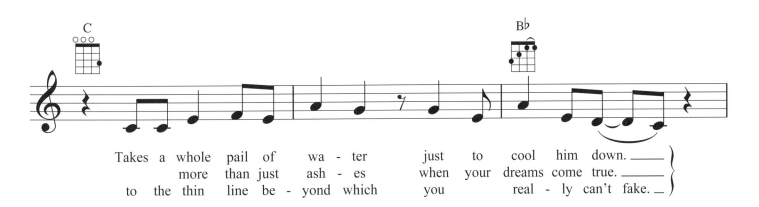

Takes a whole pail of wa - ter just to cool him down. ___ }
more than just ash - es when your dreams come true. ___ }
to the thin line be - yond which you real - ly can't fake. ___ }

Chorus

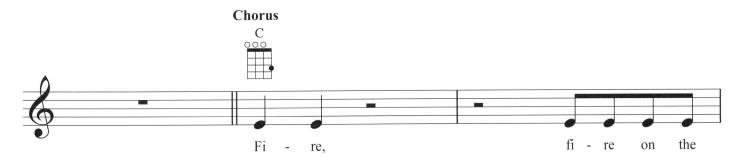

Fi - re, fi - re on the

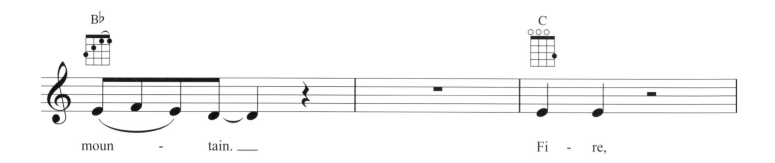

moun - tain. ___   Fi - re,

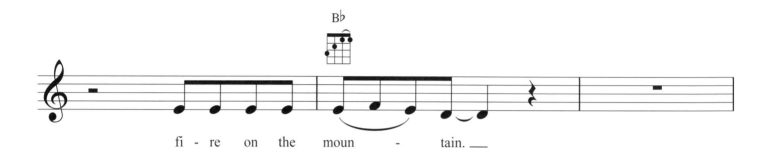

fi - re on the moun - tain. ___

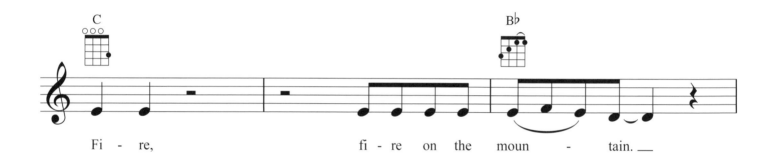

Fi - re,   fi - re on the moun - tain. ___

Fi - re,   fi - re on the

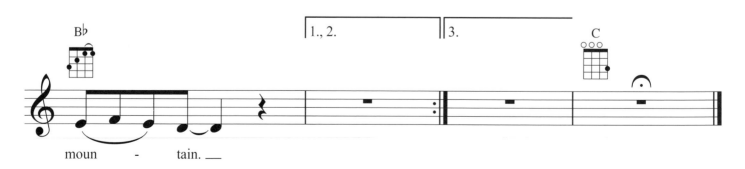

moun - tain. ___

5 Years Time

By Charlie Fink

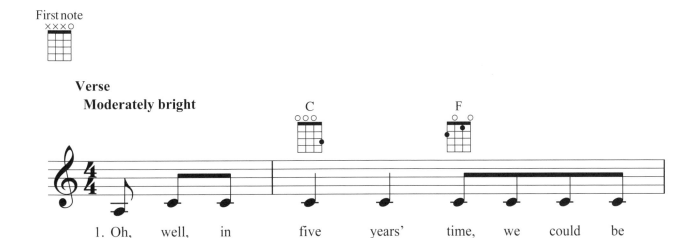

Verse
Moderately bright

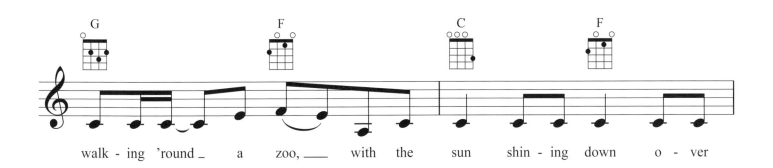

1. Oh, well, in five years' time, we could be

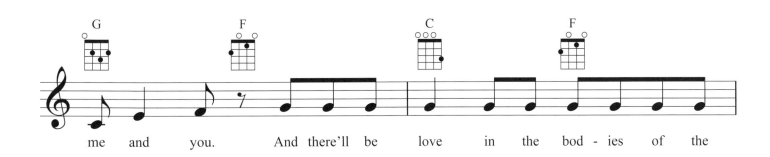

walk - ing 'round ___ a zoo, ___ with the sun shin - ing down o - ver

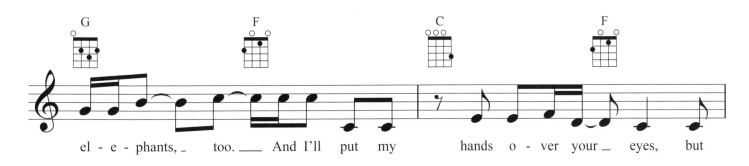

me and you. And there'll be love in the bod - ies of the

el - e - phants, ___ too. ___ And I'll put my hands o - ver your ___ eyes, but

to smoke _ all those stu - pid lit - tle cig - a - rettes and

drink stu - pid wine, _ 'cause it's what we need-ed to have a good time. _ But it was

Chorus

fun, fun, fun when we were drink-ing. It was fun, fun, fun

when we were drunk. _ And it _____ was fun, fun, fun _____

when we were laugh - ing. It was fun, fun, fun, _____

Interlude

oh, it was fun. _

Verse

3. Oh, well, I'll look at you and say, ___ "It's the hap - pi - est that

I've ev - er been." ___ And I'll say, "I no long - er feel ___ I have to be ___

___ James Dean." ___ And she'll say, "Yeah, well, I feel, oh,

pret - ty hap - py, too, ___ and I'm al - ways pret - ty hap - py when I'm ___ just

Chorus

kick - in' back ___ with you." And it - 'll be love, love, love

all through our bod - ies, and love, love, love

Folsom Prison Blues

Words and Music by John R. Cash

First note

Verse
Moderately, in 2

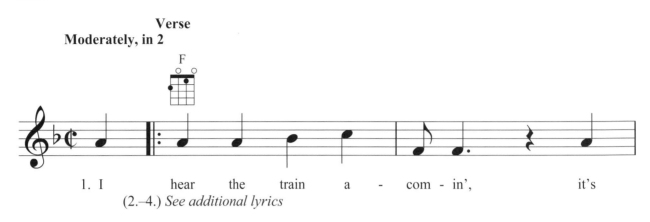

1. I hear the train a - com - in', it's
(2.–4.) *See additional lyrics*

roll - in' 'round the bend, ___ and I ain't seen the sun -

- shine since I don't ___ know when. I'm

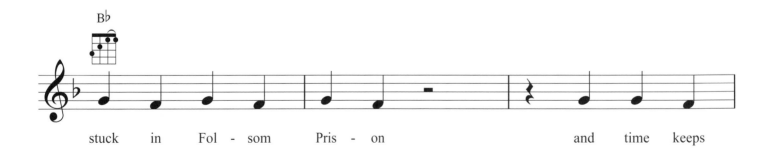

stuck in Fol - som Pris - on and time keeps

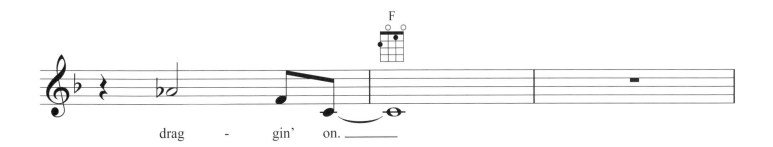

drag - gin' on. _____

But that train keeps a roll -

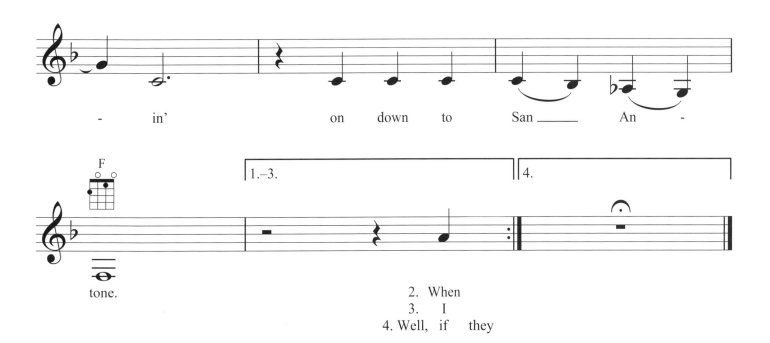

- in' on down to San _____ An -

tone.

1.–3.

4.

2. When
3. I
4. Well, if they

Additional Lyrics

2. When I was just a baby, my mama told me, "Son,
   Always be a good boy; don't ever play with guns."
   But I shot a man in Reno, just to watch him die.
   When I hear that whistle blowin', I hang my head and cry.

3. I bet there's rich folks eatin' in a fancy dining car.
   They're prob'ly drinkin' coffee and smokin' big cigars.
   Well, I know I had it comin', I know I can't be free.
   But those people keep a-movin' and that's what tortures me.

4. Well, if they freed me from this prison, if that railroad train was mine,
   I bet I'd move it on a little farther down the line.
   Far from Folsom Prison, that's where I want to stay,
   And I'd let that lonesome whistle blow my blues away.

For What It's Worth

Words and Music by Stephen Stills

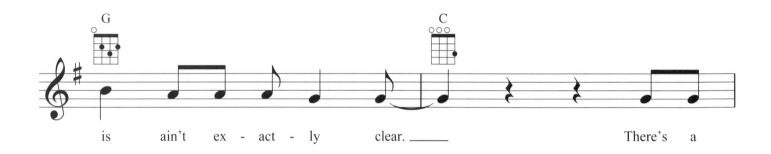

1. There's some-thing hap-pen-ing here, ____ but what it
2.– 4. *See additional lyrics*

is ain't ex-act-ly clear. ____ There's a

man with a gun o-ver there ____ tell-ing

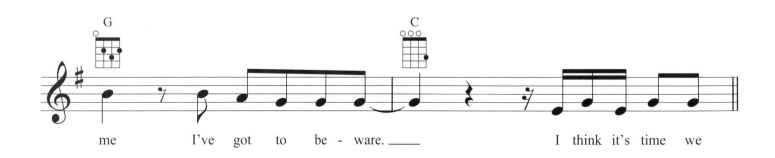

me I've got to be-ware. ____ I think it's time we

Chorus

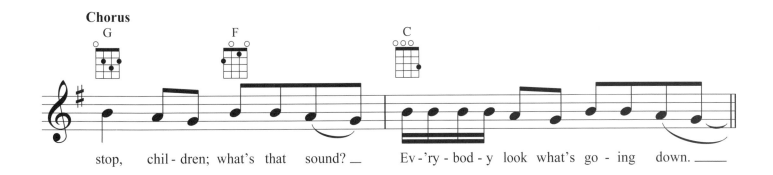

stop, chil - dren; what's that sound? __ Ev -'ry - bod - y look what's go - ing down. ____

1.–3.
Interlude

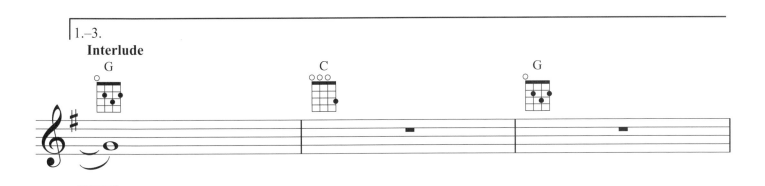

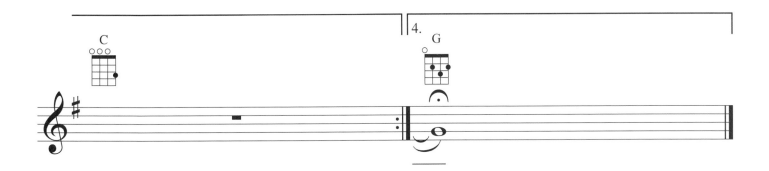

Additional Lyrics

2. There's battle lines being drawn.
   Nobody's right if everybody's wrong.
   Young people speaking their minds,
   Getting so much resistance from behind.
Chorus: I think it's time we stop; hey, what's that sound?
   Ev'rybody look what's going down.

3. What a field day for the heat.
   A thousand people in the street
   Singing songs and carrying signs,
   Mostly say, "Hooray for our side."
Chorus: It's time we stop; hey, what's that sound?
   Ev'rybody look what's going down.

4. Paranoia strikes deep.
   Into your life it will creep.
   It starts when you're always afraid.
   You step out of line, the man come and take you away.
Chorus: We better stop; hey, what's that sound?
   Ev'rybody look what's going down.

Green Green Grass of Home

Words and Music by Curly Putman

First note

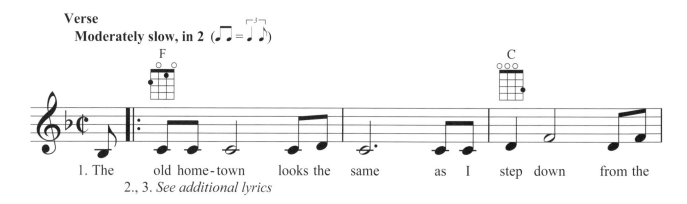

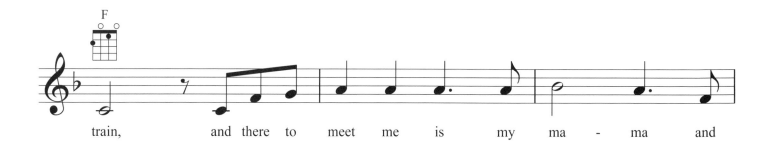

green, green grass ___ of home. _____ Yes, they'll

Chorus

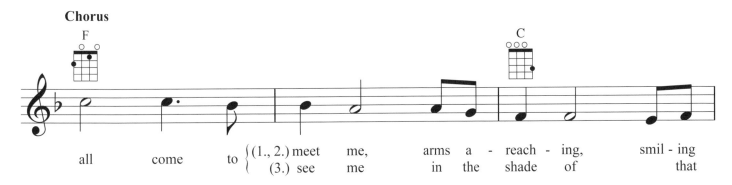

all come to {(1., 2.) meet me, arms a - reach - ing, smil - ing
(3.) see me in the shade of that

sweet - ly. It's good to touch} the green, green grass ___ of
old oak tree as they lay me 'neath}

| 1., 2. | 3. |

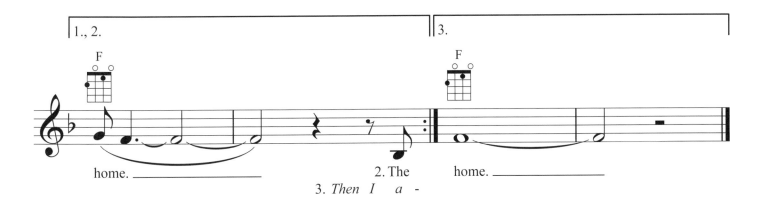

home. _____ 2. The home. _____
3. *Then I a -*

Additional Lyrics

2. The old house is still standing, though the paint is cracked and dry.
   And there's that old oak tree that I used to play on.
   Down the lane I walk with my sweet Mary, hair of gold and lips like cherries.
   It's good to touch the green, green grass of home.

3. *(Spoken:) Then I awake, and look around me at four gray walls that surround me,*
   And I realize that I was only dreaming.
   For there's a guard and there's a sad, old padre. Arm in arm we'll walk at daybreak.
   Again I'll touch the green, green grass of home.

Happy Birthday to You

Words and Music by Mildred J. Hill and Patty S. Hill

First note

Chorus
Brightly

Hap - py birth - day to you, hap - py birth - day to you. Hap - py

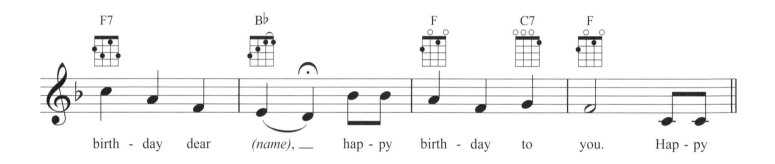

birth - day dear (name), __ hap - py birth - day to you. Hap - py

Chorus

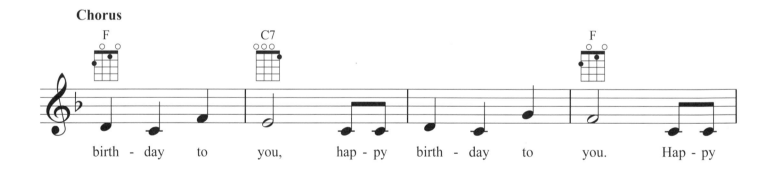

birth - day to you, hap - py birth - day to you. Hap - py

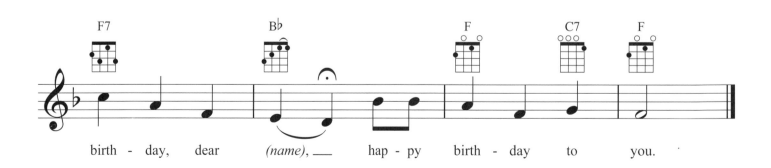

birth - day, dear (name), __ hap - py birth - day to you.

Ho Hey

Words and Music by Jeremy Fraites and Wesley Schultz

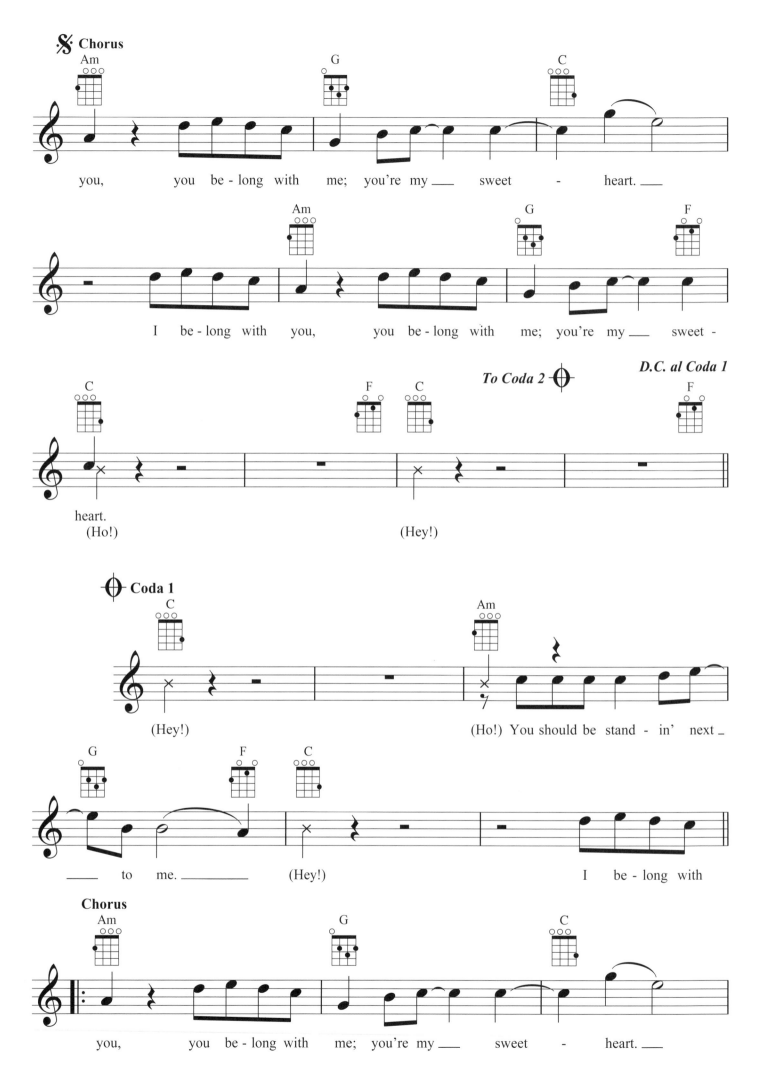

Additional Lyrics

2. (Ho!) So show me, family,
   (Hey!) All the blood that I will bleed.
   (Ho!) I don't know where I belong,
   (Hey!) I don't know where I went wrong,
   (Ho!) But I can write a song.
   (Hey!)

3. (Ho!) I don't think you're right for him.
   (Hey!) Look at what it might have been if you
   (Ho!) Took a bus to Chinatown.
   (Hey!) I'd be standing on Canal
   (Ho!) And Bowery. *(To Coda 1)*

Have You Ever Seen the Rain?

Words and Music by John Fogerty

First note

Verse
Moderately bright

1. Some-one told me long ___ a - go ___ there's a calm be - fore ___
2. Yes - ter - day and days ___ be - fore, ___ sun is cold and rain ___

___ the storm. ___ I know; ___ it's been com - in' for ___
___ is hard. ___ I know; ___ been that way ___ for all ___

___ some time. ___ When it's o - ver, so ___
___ my time. ___ Till for - ev - er, on ___

___ they say, ___ it - 'll rain a sun - ny day. ___ I know; ___
___ it goes ___ through the cir - cle, fast ___ and slow. ___ I know; ___

shin - in' down _ like wa - ter.
and it can't stop, _ I won-der.

Chorus

I _____ wan-na know: ___ have you ev - er _____ seen the

rain? I _____ wan - na know: ___ have you

ev - er _____ seen the rain com - in' down _

To Coda

2nd time, D.S. al Coda

___ on a sun - ny day? ____

Coda

___

He's Got the Whole World in His Hands

Traditional Spiritual

First note

Verse
Moderately

1. He's got the whole world __ in His hands. __ He's got the

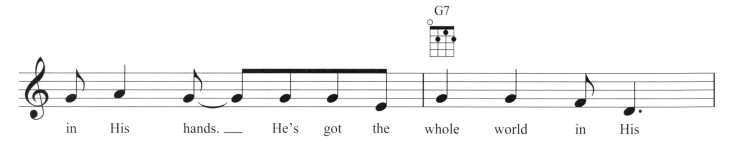

whole world __ in His hands. __ He's got the whole world __

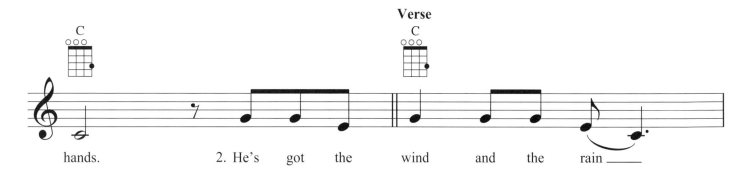

in His hands. __ He's got the whole world in His

Verse

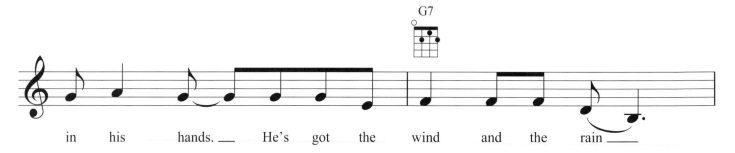

hands. 2. He's got the wind and the rain ____

in his hands. __ He's got the wind and the rain ____

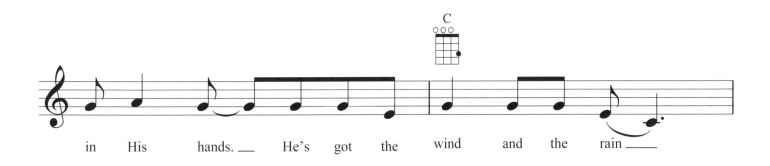

in His hands. ___ He's got the wind and the rain ___

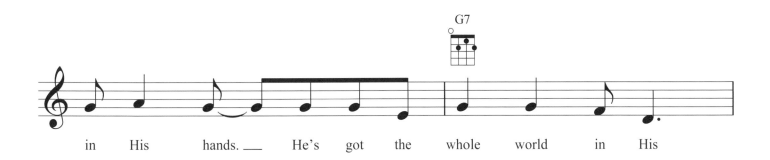

in His hands. ___ He's got the whole world in His

Verse

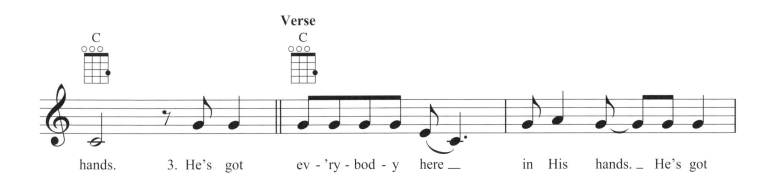

hands. 3. He's got ev - 'ry - bod - y here ___ in His hands. ___ He's got

ev - 'ry - bod - y here ___ in His hands. ___ He's got ev - 'ry - bod - y here ___

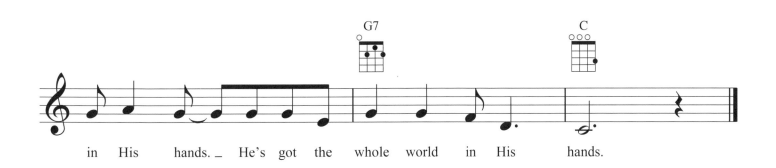

in His hands. ___ He's got the whole world in His hands.

How Much Is That Doggie in the Window

Words and Music by Bob Merrill

First note

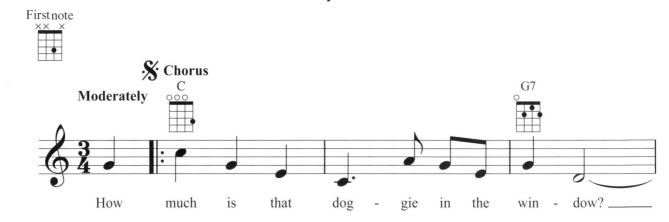

How much is that dog - gie in the win - dow? _____

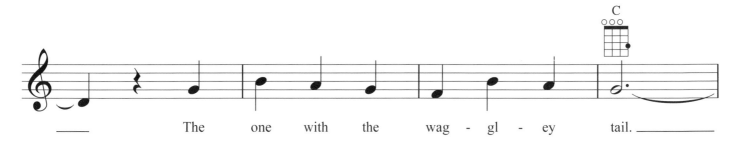

_____ The one with the wag - gl - ey tail. _____

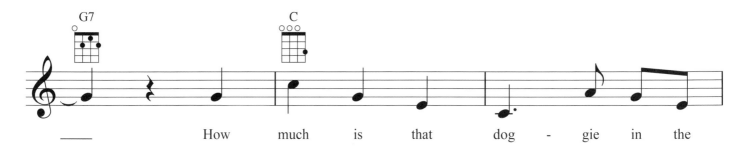

_____ How much is that dog - gie in the

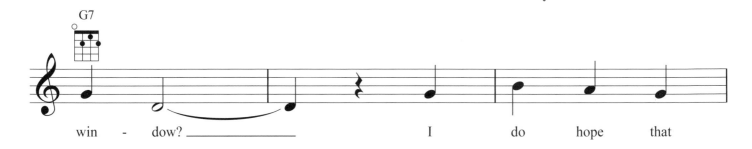

win - dow? _____ I do hope that

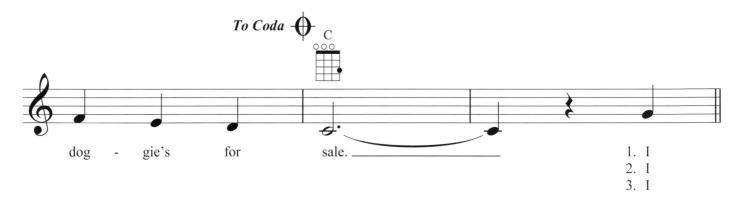

dog - gie's for sale. _____

1. I
2. I
3. I

Copyright © 1952 Golden Bell Songs
Copyright Renewed 1980
Administered by Music & Media International, Inc.
International Copyright Secured   All Rights Reserved

I Saw the Light

Words and Music by Hank Williams

First note

Verse

Lively, in 2

1. I wan-dered so aim-less, life filled with

2., 3. *See additional lyrics*

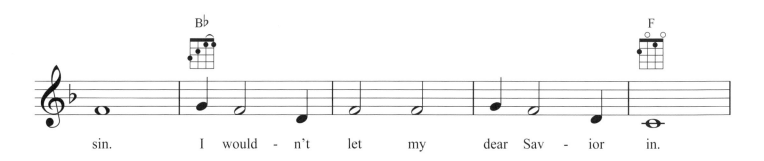

sin. I would-n't let my dear Sav-ior in.

Then Je-sus came like a stran-ger in the night.

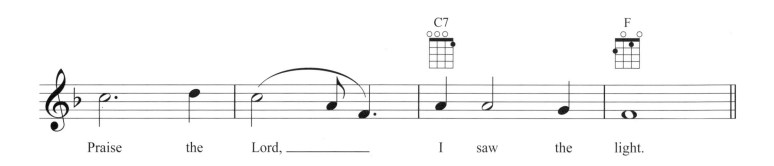

Praise the Lord, _____ I saw the light.

Chorus

I saw the light, _____ I saw the light, _____

no more _____ dark - ness, no more night. _____ Now I'm so

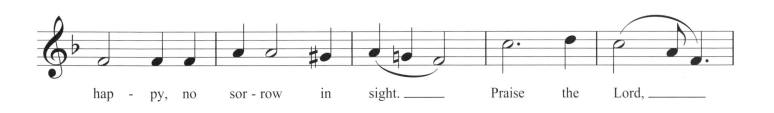

hap - py, no sor - row in sight. _____ Praise the Lord, _____

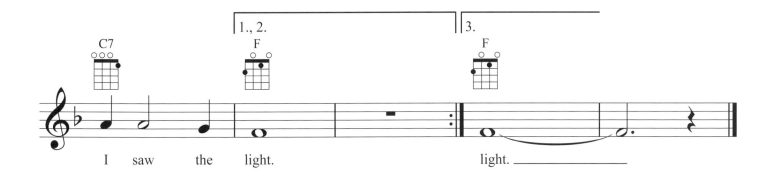

I saw the light.   light. _____

Additional Lyrics

2. Just like a blind man I wandered along,
   Worries and fears I claimed for my own.
   Then like the blind man that God gave back his sight,
   Praise the Lord, I saw the light.

3. I was a fool to wander and stray,
   Straight is the gate and narrow is the way.
   Now I have traded the wrong for the right.
   Praise the Lord, I saw the light.

I Still Haven't Found What I'm Looking For

Words and Music by U2

First note

Moderately

Verse

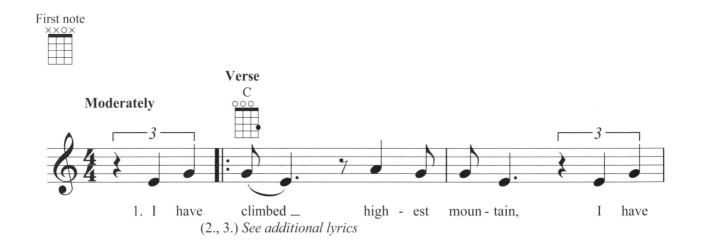

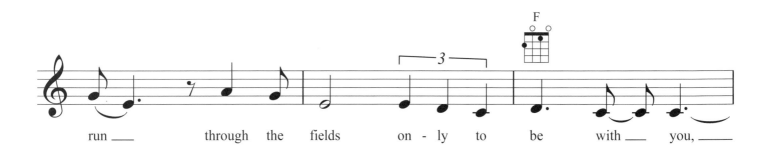

1. I have climbed __ high-est moun-tain, I have

(2., 3.) *See additional lyrics*

run __ through the fields on-ly to be with __ you, __

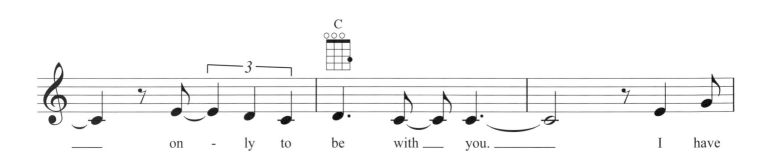

__ on-ly to be with __ you. __ I have

run, __ I have crawled, I have scaled __ these cit-

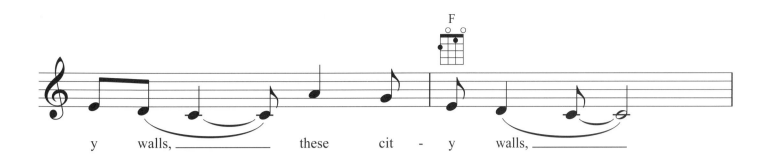

y walls, _____ these cit - y walls, _____

on - ly to be with ___ you. _____ But I still ___

Chorus

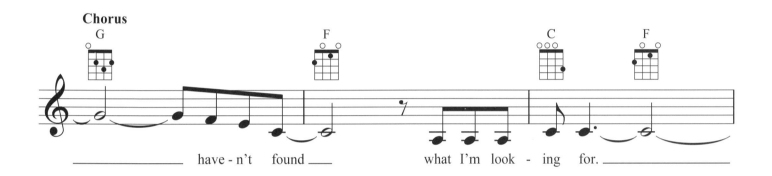

_____ have - n't found ___ what I'm look - ing for. _____

___ But I still _____ have - n't found ___ what I'm look -

ing for. _____ 2. I have ___ But I still ___
3. I be -

Outro-Chorus

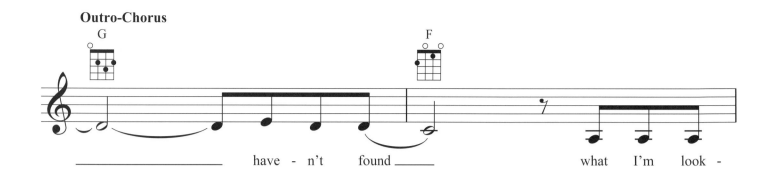

have - n't found _____ what I'm look -

ing for. _____ But I still _____ have - n't found _

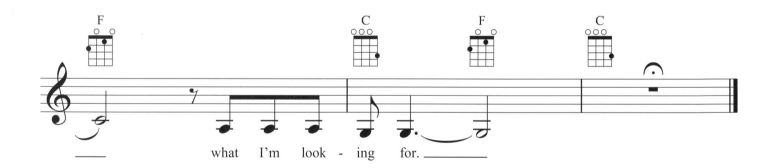

_____ what I'm look - ing for. _____

Additional Lyrics

2. I have kissed honey lips, felt the healing fingertips.
   It burned like fire, this burning desire.
   I have spoke with the tongue of angels, I have held the hand of the devil.
   It was warm in the night, I was cold as a stone.

3. I believe in the kingdom come, then all the colors will bleed into one,
   Bleed into one. But, yes, I'm still runnin'.
   You broke the bonds and you loosed the chains, carried the cross of my shame,
   Of my shame. You know I believe it.

Hush, Little Baby

Carolina Folk Lullaby

I'm Yours

Words and Music by Jason Mraz

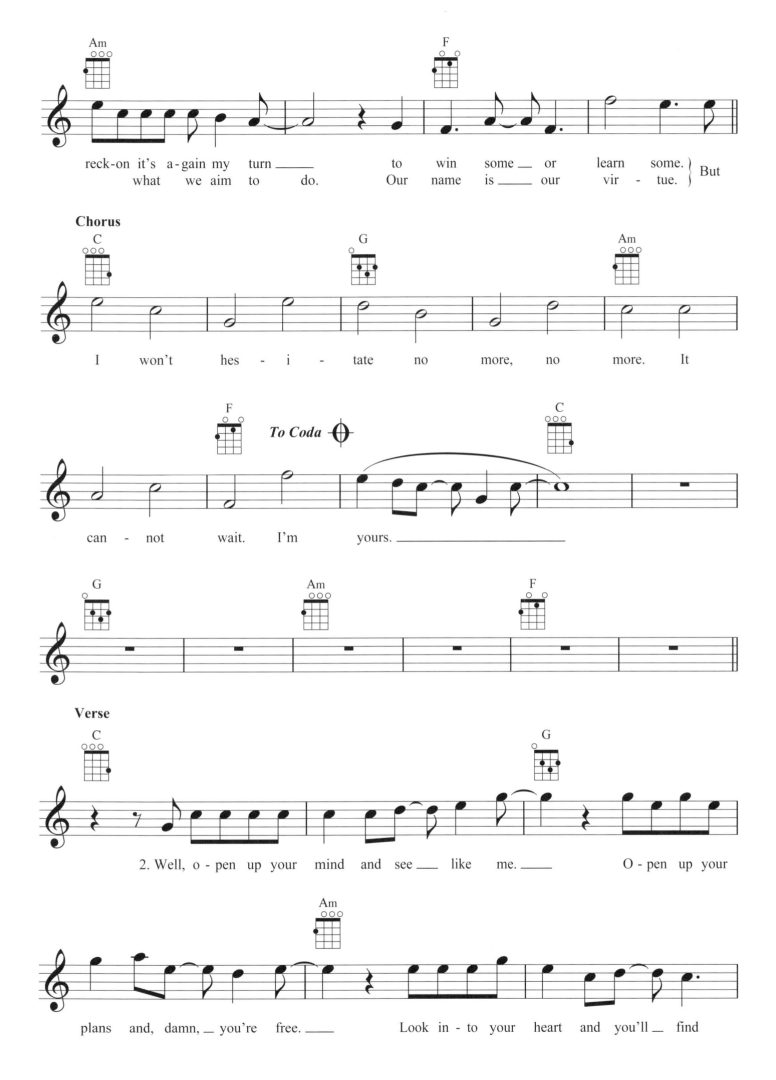

reck-on it's a-gain my turn _____ to win some __ or learn some. ⎫
what we aim to do. Our name is _____ our vir - tue. ⎬ But

Chorus

I won't hes - i - tate no more, no more. It

To Coda ⊕

can - not wait. I'm yours. _____

Verse

2. Well, o - pen up your mind and see __ like me. __ O - pen up your

plans and, damn, __ you're free. __ Look in - to your heart and you'll __ find

love, love, _____ love, love. Lis - ten to the mu - sic of the

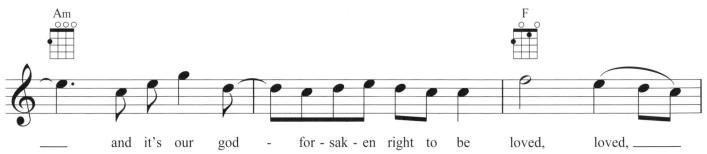

mo - ment; peo - ple dance _ and sing. We're just one big fam - i - ly, _

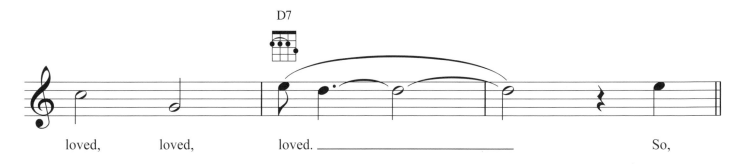

___ and it's our god - for - sak - en right to be loved, loved, _____

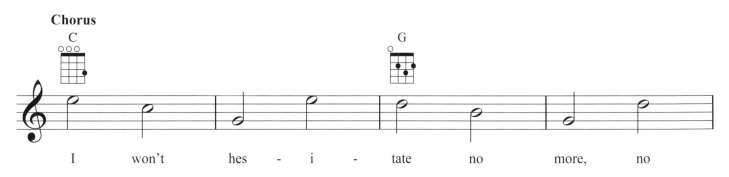

loved, loved, loved. _____ So,

Chorus

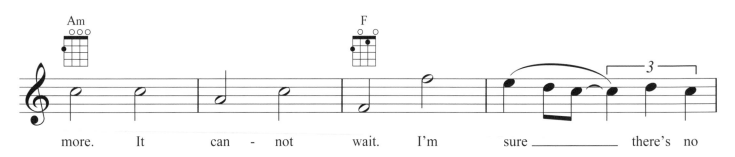

I won't hes - i - tate no more, no

more. It can - not wait. I'm sure _____ there's no

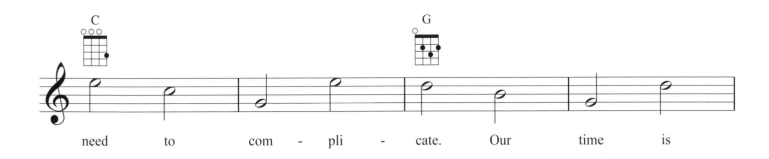

need   to   com - pli - cate.   Our   time   is

short.   This   is   our   fate.   I'm   yours. _____ *Scat...*

Interlude

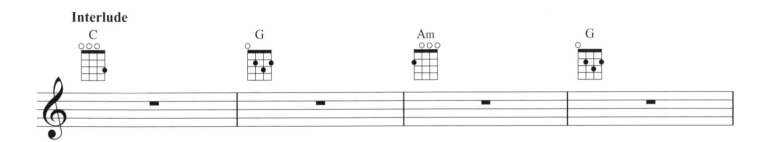

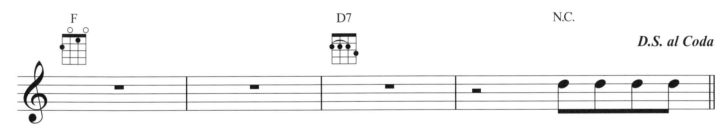

D.S. al Coda

3. I've been spend - ing

Coda

Verse/Chorus

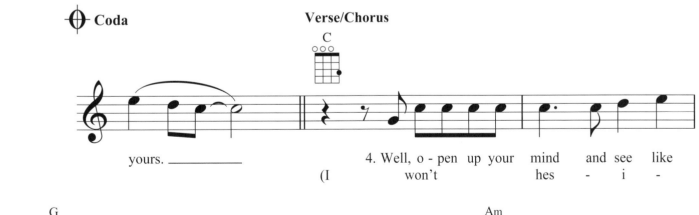

yours. _____   4. Well, o - pen up your   mind   and see   like
(I   won't   hes - i -

me.   O - pen up your   plans   and, damn, __ you're   free.   Look in - to your
tate   no   more,   no   more.   It

Kiss the Girl

from Walt Disney's THE LITTLE MERMAID

Music by Alan Menken
Lyrics by Howard Ashman

First note

Verse
Moderate Calypso feel

1. There you see ___ her, sit-ting there a - cross the way. ___
2. Yes, you want ___ her. Look at her; you know you do. ___

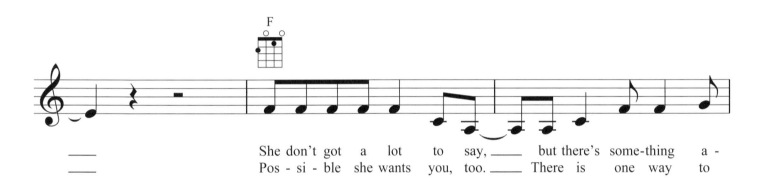

___ She don't got a lot to say, ___ but there's some-thing a -
___ Pos - si - ble she wants you, too. ___ There is one way to

bout her. And you don't know why, ___ but you're
ask her. It don't take a word, ___ not a

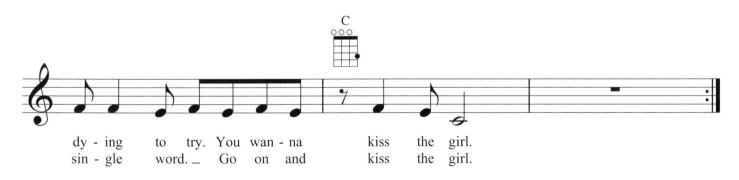

dy - ing to try. You wan - na kiss the girl.
sin - gle word. ___ Go on and kiss the girl.

Chorus

Sha la la la la la, my oh my. __ Look like the boy too shy. __ Ain't gon-na

kiss the girl. Sha la la la la la, ain't that sad. __ Ain't it a

shame, too bad. __ He gon-na miss the girl. __ *(Instrumental)*

Verse

3. Now's your mo - ment, float-ing in a blue la - goon. __

__ Boy, you bet - ter do it soon. __ No time will be

bet - ter. __ She don't say a word __ and she won't __

It's a Small World

from Disneyland Resort® and Magic Kingdom® Park
Words and Music by Richard M. Sherman and Robert B. Sherman

Keep on the Sunny Side

Words and Music by A.P. Carter

First note

Verse

Moderately, in 2

1. There's a dark and a trou-bled side of life;
(2.) storm and its fu-ry broke to-day,
(3.) greet with a song of hope each day,

there's a bright and a sun-ny side, too.
crush-ing hopes that we cher-ish so dear.
though the mo-ment be cloud-y or fair.

Though you meet with the dark-ness and strife,
Clouds and storms will in time pass a-way;
Let us trust in our Sav-ior a-way,

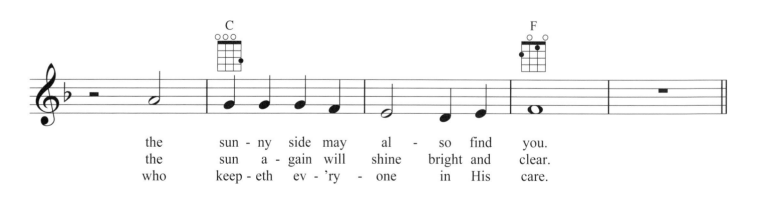

the sun-ny side may al-so find you.
the sun a-gain will shine bright and clear.
who keep-eth ev-'ry-one in His care.

Chorus

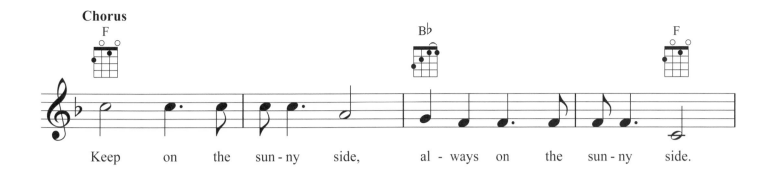

Keep   on   the   sun - ny   side,   al - ways   on   the   sun - ny   side.

Keep   on   the   sun - ny   side   of   life.   It   will

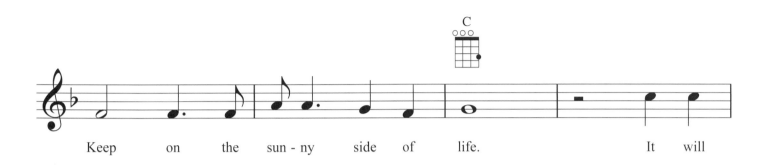

help   us   ev - 'ry   day,   it   will   bright - en   all ____ the

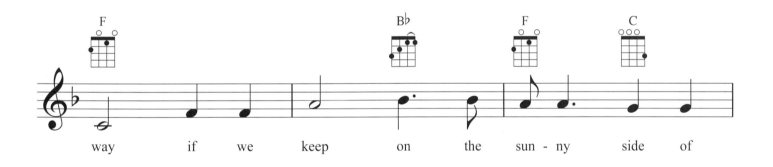

way   if   we   keep   on   the   sun - ny   side   of

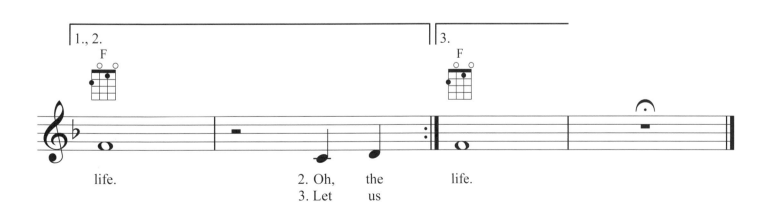

life.   2. Oh,   the   life.
          3. Let   us

King of the Road

Words and Music by Roger Miller

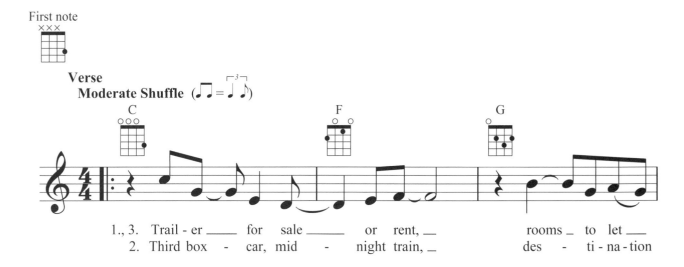

1., 3. Trail - er ___ for sale ___ or rent, ___ rooms _ to let ___
2. Third box - car, mid - night train, ___ des - ti - na - tion

fif - ty cents. ___ No phone, ___ no pool, ___ no pets. ___
Ban - gor, Maine. _ Old worn - out suit ___ and shoes, ___

I ain't got no cig - a - rettes, ___ ah, but two hours ___ of
I don't pay no un - ion dues. ___ I smoke old sto - gies

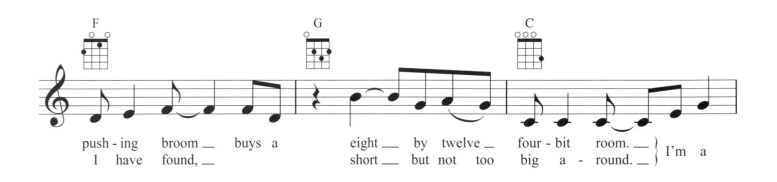

push - ing broom ___ buys a eight ___ by twelve _ four - bit room. ___ } I'm a
I have found, ___ short ___ but not too big a - round. ___

man   of   means ___   by   no   means,   king   of   the   road. ___

___   ___   I know   ev - er - y   en - gi - neer on

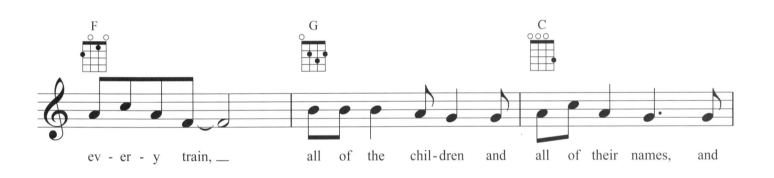

ev - er - y   train, ___   all of the chil - dren and all of their names,   and

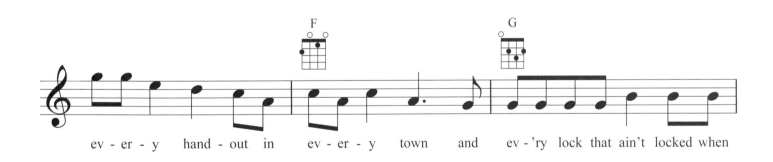

ev - er - y   hand - out in   ev - er - y   town   and ev - 'ry lock that ain't locked when

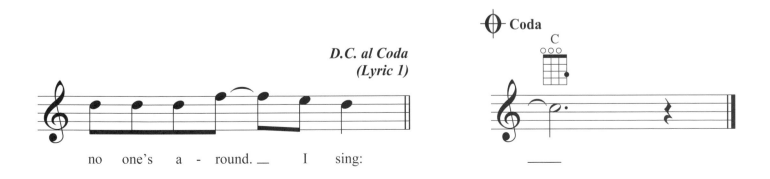

no one's a - round. ___   I   sing: ___

La Bamba

By Ritchie Valens

First note

Pa - ra bai - lar la bam - ba, pa - ra bai - lar la bam-

- ba se ne - ce - si - ta u - na po - ca de gra - cia.

U - na po - ca de gra - cia par' mi par' ti _____ y ar - ri bay ar - ri-

- ba, ar - ri - bay ar - ri - ba. Por ti se - ré, _____

_____ por ti se - ré, por ti se - ré. Yo no soy ma - ri-

Lava

from LAVA
Music and Lyrics by James Ford Murphy

Male: 1. A long, long time a-go, ___ there was a
2. But lit-tle did he know ___ that, liv-ing in the

vol-ca-no ___ liv-ing all a-lone ___ in the
sea be-low, ___ an-oth-er vol-ca-no ___ was ___

mid-dle of ___ the sea. He sat high a-
lis-ten-ing to his song. Ev-'ry day she

bove his bay, ___ watch-ing all the cou-ples play ___ and
heard his tune, ___ her ___ la-va grew and grew, ___ be-cause

wish-ing that ___ he had some-one, too.
she be-lieved ___ his song was meant for her.

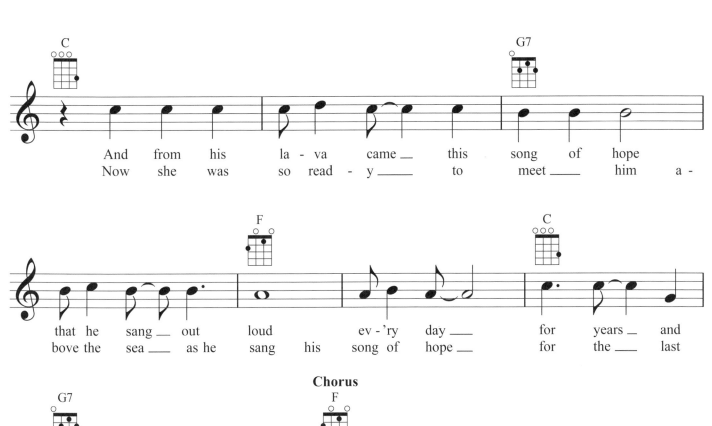

And from his la-va came ___ this song of hope
Now she was so read-y ___ to meet ___ him a-

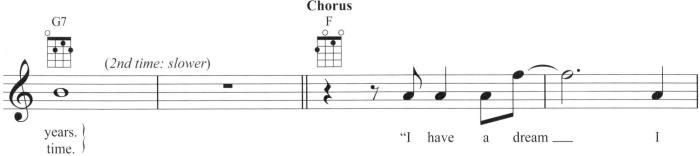

that he sang ___ out loud ev-'ry day ___ for years ___ and
bove the sea ___ as he sang his song of hope ___ for the ___ last

Chorus

(*2nd time: slower*)

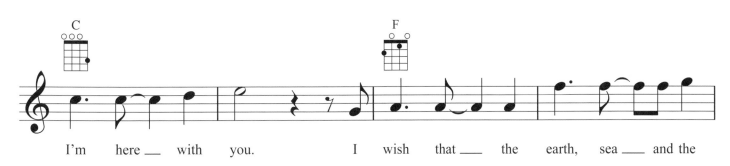

years.
time.

"I have a dream ___ I

hope will ___ come true, that you're here ___ with me and

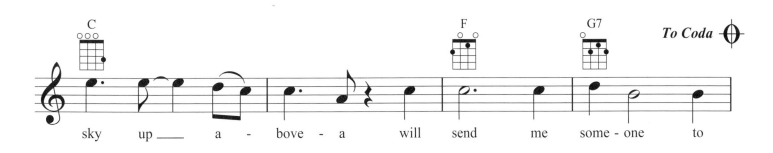

I'm here ___ with you. I wish that ___ the earth, sea ___ and the

To Coda

sky up ___ a - bove - a will send me some - one to

vol - ca - no, ___ look - ing ___ all a - round, _ but she could not ___ see

him. 4. He tried to sing to let her know __ that
(5.) filled the sea ___ with his tears __ and

she was not there a - lone, __ but with no ___ la - va his ___
watched his dreams dis - ap - pear __ as she re - mem - bered what __ his

1.

song was __ all gone. 5. He
song meant _ to

2.

slower *accel.*

her. _____

Chorus (Tempo I)

___ *Female:* "I have a dream __ I hope will __ come

true, that you're here __ with me and I'm here __ with

you. I ____ wish that ____ the earth, sea ____ and the sky up ____ a -

bove - a will send me some - one to la - va." ____

Interlude

a tempo

Verse

Male: 6. Oh, they were so hap - py ____ to fi - n'lly meet a -
(7.) long - er are they all a - lone, ____ with *a - lo - ha* ____ as

bove the sea. ____ All ____ to - geth - er now ____ their
their new home, ____ and when you vis - it them ____

la - va grew and grew. 7. No
this is what they sing.

Love Me Do

Words and Music by John Lennon and Paul McCartney

Some - one to love, some - one like you.

End instrumental

Chorus

Love, love me do, _____ you know I love you. __

____ I'll al - ways be true. ____ So

N.C.

please, _____ love me do. _____

1.

Whoa. ____ Love ____ me do. ____

2.

Whoa. _____ Love ____ me do. ____

Rude

Words and Music by Nasri Atweh, Mark Pellizzer, Alex Tanas, Ben Spivak and Adam Messinger

'cause I know that you're an old-fash-ioned man.
you know she's in love with me. She will go

Pre-Chorus

an-y-where I go. Can I have your daugh-ter for the rest of my life? Say

yes, say yes, 'cause I need to know. You say I'll nev-er get your bless-ing till the

day I die. Tough luck, my friend, { but the an-swer is no. }
{ 'cause the an-swer's still no. }

Chorus

Why you got-ta be so rude? Don't you know I'm

hu-man, too? Why you got-ta be so rude?

I'm gon - na mar - ry her an - y - way. Mar - ry that girl,

mar - ry her an - y - way. Mar - ry that girl, yeah, no mat - ter what you say.

Mar - ry that girl and we'll be a fam - i - ly. Why you got - ta

be so rude? _____

Rude. _____

Pre-Chorus

Can I have your daugh - ter for the

Run Through the Jungle

Words and Music by John Fogerty

First note

Verse
Moderately fast

1. Thought it was a night - mare;
2. Thought I heard a rum - blin',
3. O - ver on the moun - tain,

lo, it's all _____ so true. _____
call - in' to _____ my name. _____
thun - der mag - ic spoke: _____

They told me, "Don't go walk - in' slow; _____ the
Two hun - dred mil - lion guns are load - ed;
"Let the peo - ple know my wis - dom;

dev - il's on _____ the loose." _____)
Sa - tan cries, _____ "Take aim!" _____)
fill the land _____ with smoke." _____)

Bet - ter run _____

Chorus

through the jun - gle,   bet - ter run

through the jun - gle,   bet - ter run

through the jun - gle.   Whoa, don't

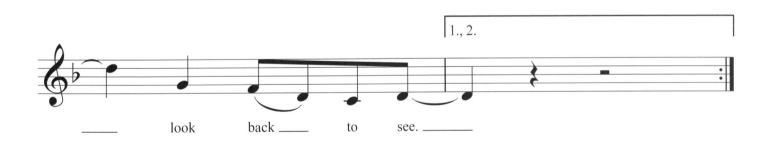

look back to see.

1., 2.

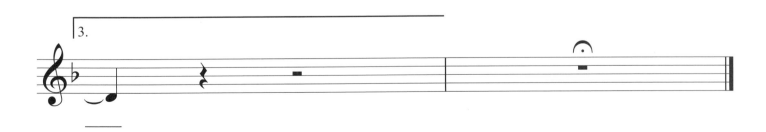

3.

Shake It Off

Words and Music by Taylor Swift, Max Martin and Shellback

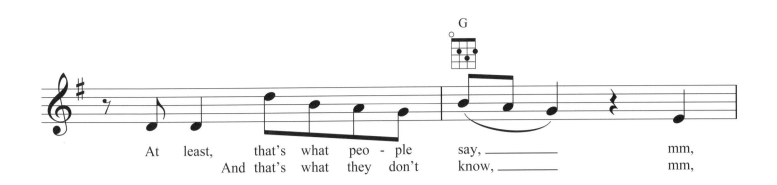

At least, that's what peo - ple say, _____ mm,
And that's what they don't know, _____ mm,

mm. That's what peo - ple say, _____ mm, mm. But I keep
mm. That's what they don't know, _____ mm, mm. But I keep

Pre-Chorus

cruis - ing; can't stop, won't stop mov - ing. } It's
cruis - ing; can't stop, won't stop groov - ing. } It's

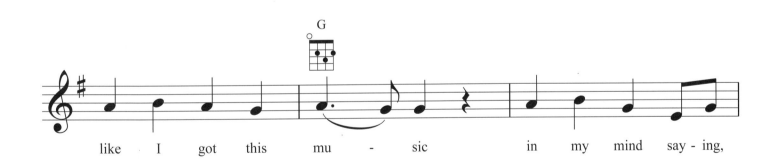

like I got this mu - sic in my mind say - ing,

"It's gon - na be al - right." _____ 'Cause the

play - ers gon - na play, play, play, play, play and the hat - ers gon - na hate, hate,

hate, hate, hate, ba - by. I'm just gon - na shake, shake, shake, shake, shake; _ I

shake it off, I shake it off.   Heart - break - ers gon - na break, break,
(Ooh, _____ ooh!)

break, break, break and the fak - ers gon - na fake, fake, fake, fake, fake, ba - by.

To Coda ⊕

I'm just gon - na shake, shake, shake, shake, shake; _ I shake it off, I shake it

off. 2. I nev-er miss a   off. (Ooh, _____ ooh!) I   shake it off,   I shake it
(Ooh, _____ ooh!)

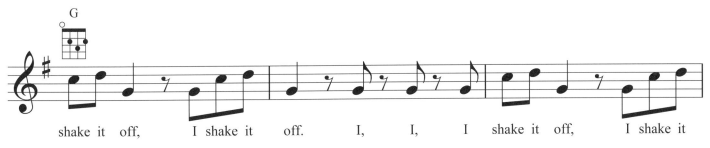

off.   I,   I,   I shake it off,   I shake it   off.   I,   I,   I

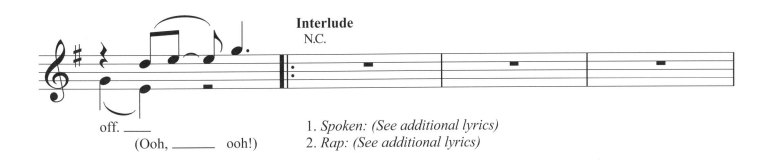

shake it off,   I shake it   off.   I,   I,   I   shake it off,   I shake it

off. _____
(Ooh, _____ ooh!)

1. *Spoken: (See additional lyrics)*
2. *Rap: (See additional lyrics)*

Rap ends   Yeah, _____ oh. _____ 'Cause the

off. (Ooh, _____ ooh!) I shake it off, I shake it

off. I, I, I shake it off, I shake it off. I, I, I

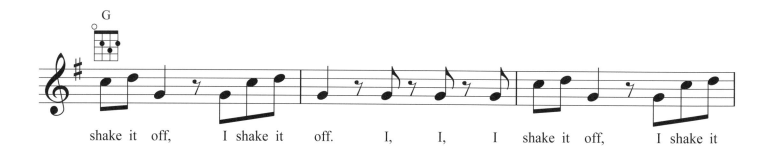

shake it off, I shake it off. I, I, I shake it off, I shake it

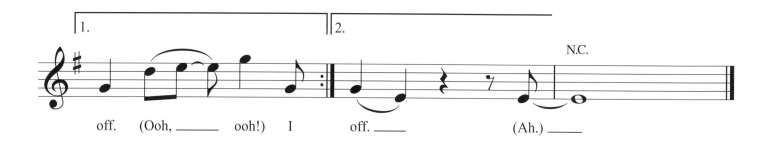

off. (Ooh, _____ ooh!) I   off. _____   (Ah.) _____

Additional Lyrics

Spoken: Hey, hey, hey! Just think: While you've been gettin'
Down and out about the liars and the dirty, dirty cheats of the world,
You could've been gettin' down to this sick beat!

Rap: My ex-man brought his new girlfriend.
She's like, "Oh, my god!" But I'm just gonna shake.
And to the fella over there with the hella good hair,
Won't you come on over, baby? We can shake, shake, shake.

Release Me

Words and Music by Robert Yount, Eddie Miller and Dub Williams

Something in the Way

Words and Music by Kurt Cobain

First note

Verse
Slowly, in 2

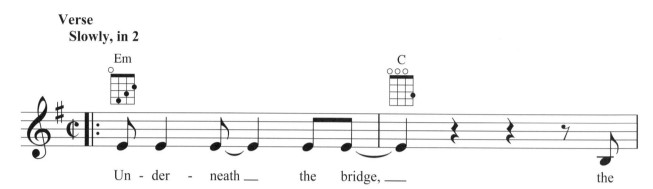

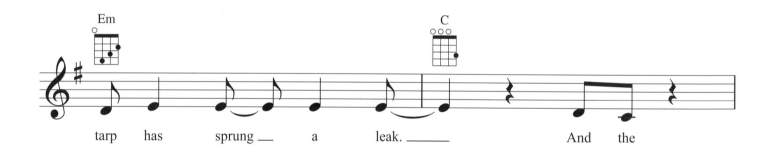

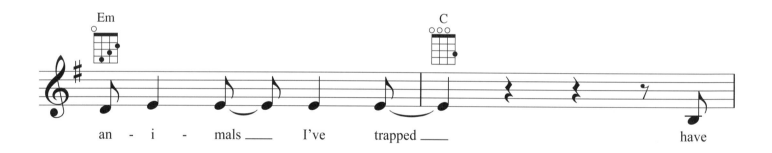

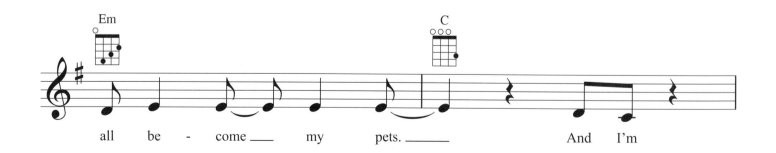

liv - ing off ____ of grass ____ and the drip - pings from __ the ceil -

\- ing. It's o - kay ___ to eat fish, ____ 'cause they

Chorus

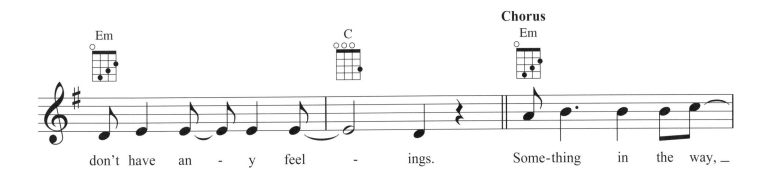

don't have an - y feel - ings. Some-thing in the way, _

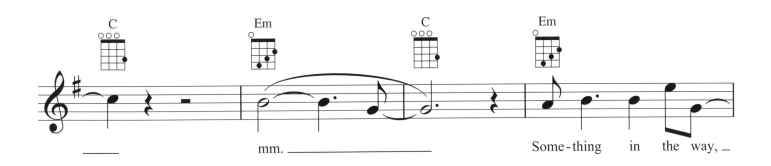

____ mm. _____ Some-thing in the way, _

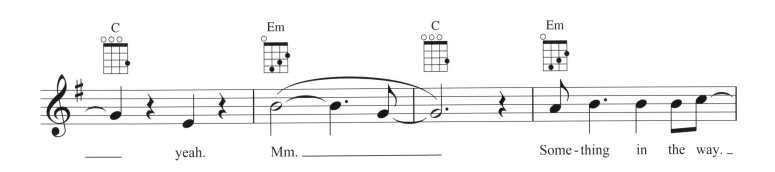

____ yeah. Mm. _____ Some-thing in the way. _

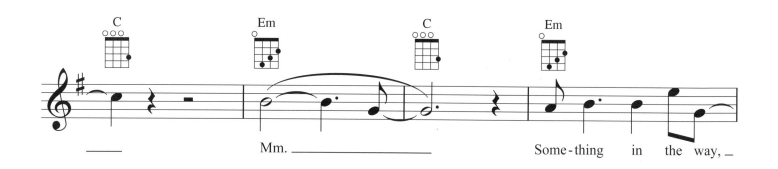

_____ Mm. _____ Some-thing in the way, __

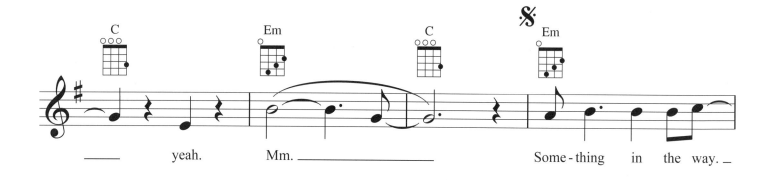

____ yeah. Mm. _____ Some-thing in the way. _

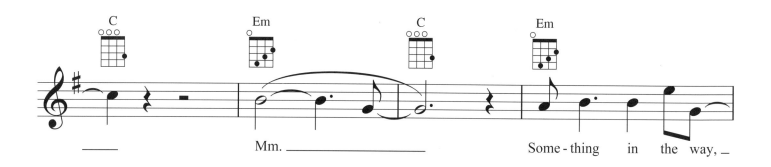

____ Mm. _____ Some-thing in the way, _

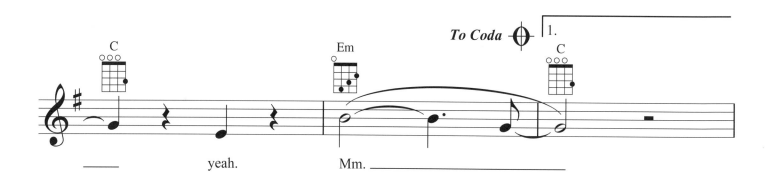

To Coda 1.

____ yeah. Mm. _____

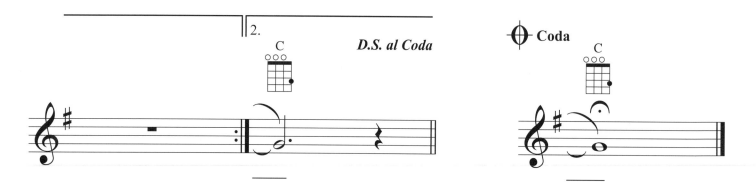

2. *D.S. al Coda* Coda

Stand by Me

Words and Music by Jerry Leiber, Mike Stoller and Ben E. King

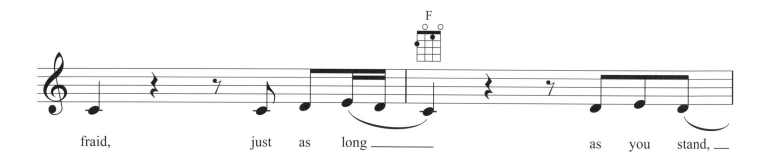

fraid,   just   as   long _____   as   you   stand, __

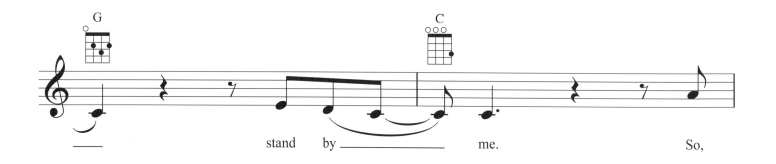

__   stand   by _____   me.   So,

Chorus

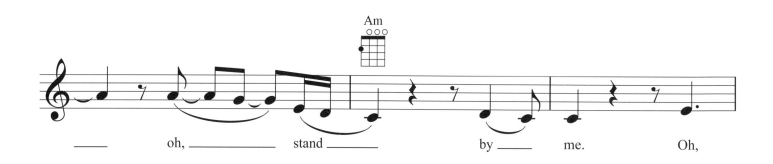

dar - lin',   dar - lin',   stand _____   by   me, __

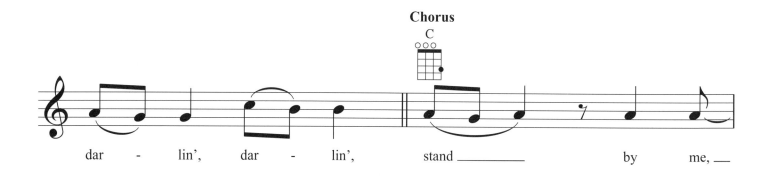

__   oh, _____   stand _____   by __   me.   Oh,

stand, __   stand   by __   me,   stand   by __   me.

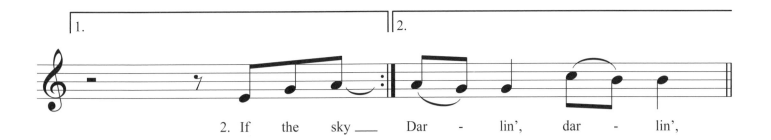

2. If the sky ___ Dar - lin', dar - lin',

Outro-Chorus

stand _____ by me, _____ oh, _____ stand _____

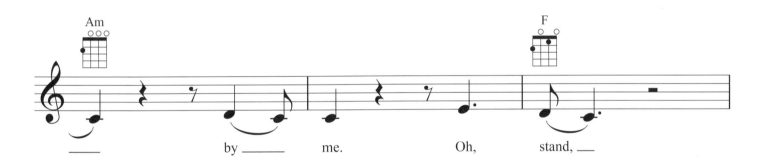

___ by _____ me. Oh, stand, ___

stand by ___ me, stand by ___ me.

Additional Lyrics

2. If the sky that we look upon should tumble and fall,
Or the mountains should crumble to the sea,
I won't cry, I won't cry. No, I won't shed a tear,
Just as long as you stand, stand by me.
And darlin', darlin'... (*To Chorus*)

Stay with Me

Words and Music by Sam Smith, James Napier, William Edward Phillips, Tom Petty and Jeff Lynne

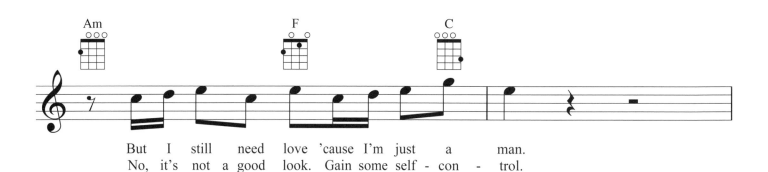

1. Guess it's true, I'm not good at a one-night stand.
2. Why am I so e-mo-tion-al?

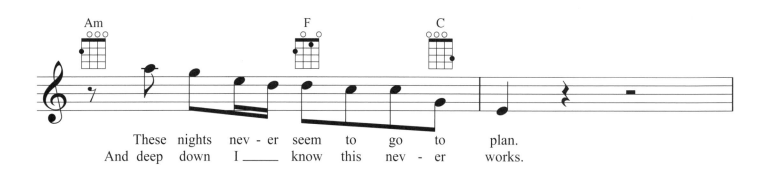

But I still need love 'cause I'm just a man.
No, it's not a good look. Gain some self-con-trol.

These nights nev-er seem to go to plan.
And deep down I ___ know this nev-er works.

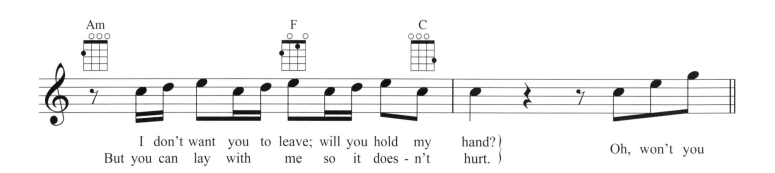

I don't want you to leave; will you hold my hand?}
But you can lay with me so it does-n't hurt.}

Oh, won't you

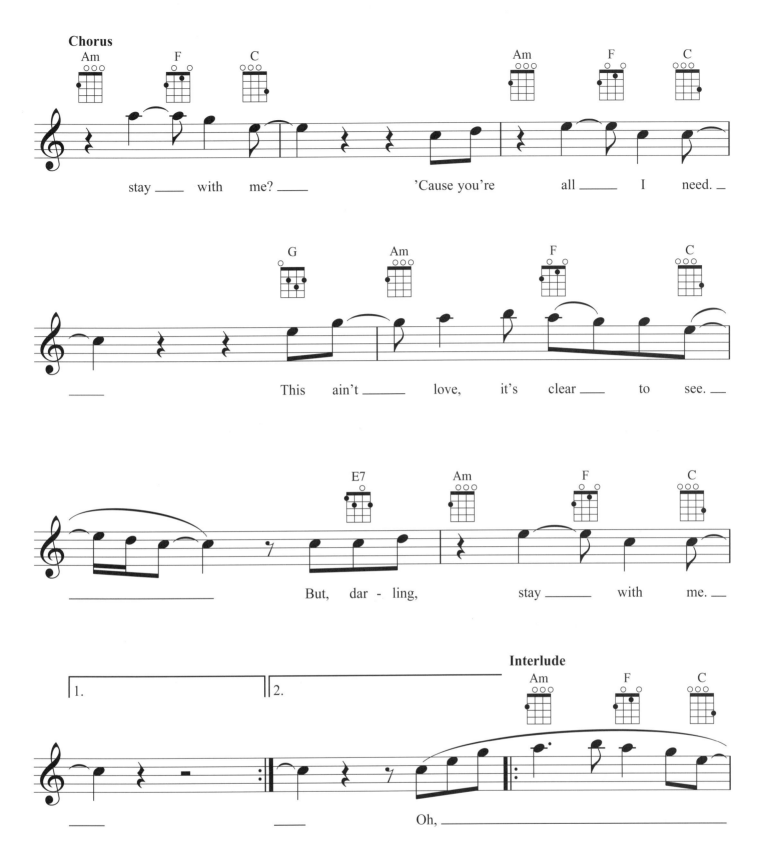

Chorus

stay ____ with me? ____ 'Cause you're all ____ I need. _

____ This ain't ____ love, it's clear ____ to see. _

_____ But, dar - ling, stay _____ with me. __

Interlude

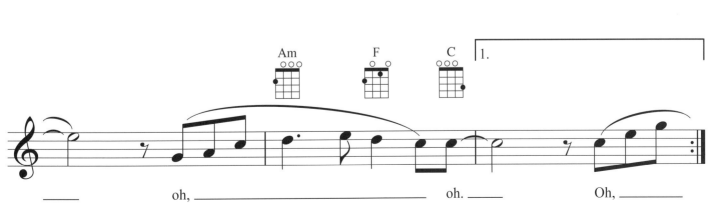

1.

2.

___ ___ Oh, _____

___ oh, _____ oh. Oh, _____

1.

Outro-Chorus

_ Oh, won't you   stay _____ with   me? _

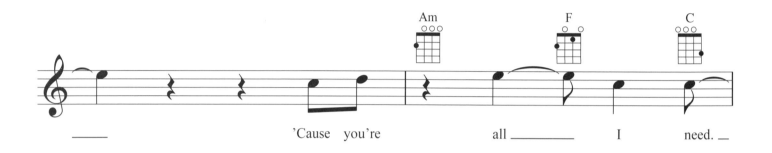

_ 'Cause you're   all _____ I   need. _

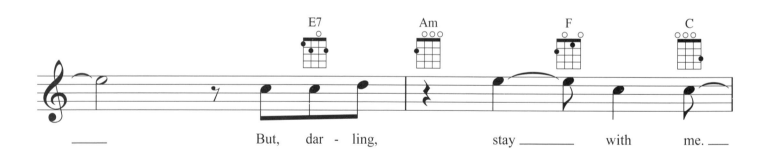

_ This   ain't _____ love,   it's   clear ___ to   see. _

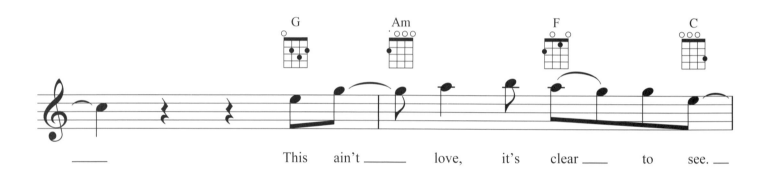

_ But,   dar - ling,   stay _____ with   me. _

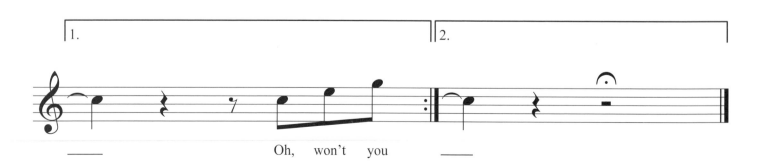

_ Oh,   won't   you _

Supercalifragilisticexpialidocious

from Walt Disney's MARY POPPINS
Words and Music by Richard M. Sherman and Robert B. Sherman

Sweet Home Alabama

Words and Music by Ronnie Van Zant, Ed King and Gary Rossington

D.S. al Coda

Additional Lyrics

2. Well, I heard Mr. Young sing about her.
Well, I heard ol' Neil put her down.
Well, I hope Neil Young will remember
A southern man don't need him around anyhow.

4. Now, Muscle Shoals has got the Swampers,
And they've been known to pick a tune or two.
Lord, they get me off so much.
They pick me up when I'm feeling blue.
(Now, how 'bout you?)

The Wreck of the Edmund Fitzgerald

Words and Music by Gordon Lightfoot

1. The leg - end lives __ on __ from the Chip - pe - wa on
2.–14. *See additional lyrics*

down of the big lake they call "Git - che Gu - mee."

The lake, it is __ said, __

__ nev - er __ gives up her dead __ when the skies __ of No -

vem - ber turn gloom - y.

14. G

Outro G

2. With a ear - ly." *(Instrumental)*

Dm F

G F

C

G

Repeat and fade

Additional Lyrics

2. With a load of iron ore twenty-six thousand tons more
Than the Edmund Fitzgerald weighed empty,
That good ship and true was a bone to be chewed
When the gales of November came early.

3. The ship was the pride of the American side
Coming back from some mill in Wisconsin.
As the big freighters go, it was bigger than most,
With a crew and a captain well seasoned.

(continued on next page)

4. Concluding some terms with a couple of steel firms
   When they left fully loaded for Cleveland.
   And later that night when the ship's bell rang,
   Could it be the north wind they'd been feelin'?

5. The wind in the wires made a tattletale sound
   And a wave broke over the railing.
   And ev'ry man knew, as the captain did too,
   'Twas the witch of November come stealin'.

6. The dawn came late and the breakfast had to wait
   When the gales of November came slashin'.
   When afternoon came, it was freezin' rain
   In the face of a hurricane west wind.

7. When suppertime came, the old cook came on deck
   Sayin', "Fellas, it's too rough to feed ya."
   At seven p.m. a main hatchway caved in.
   He said, "Fellas, it's been good to know ya!"

8. The captain wired in he had water comin' in
   And the good ship and crew was in peril.
   And later that night when his lights went outta sight
   Came the wreck of the Edmund Fitzgerald.

9. Does anyone know where the love of God goes
   When the waves turn the minutes to hours?
   The searchers all say they'd have made Whitefish Bay
   If they'd put fifteen more miles behind her.

10. They might have split up or they might have capsized.
    They may have broke deep and took water.
    And all that remains is the faces and the names
    Of the wives and the sons and the daughters.

11. Lake Huron rolls, Superior sings
    In the rooms of her ice-water mansion.
    Old Michigan steams like a young man's dreams;
    The islands and bays are for sportsmen.

12. And farther below, Lake Ontario
    Takes in what Lake Erie can send her.
    And the iron boats go, as the mariners all know,
    With the gales of November remembered.

13. In a musty old hall in Detroit they prayed
    In the Maritime Sailors' Cathedral.
    The church bell chimed till it rang twenty-nine times
    For each man on the Edmund Fitzgerald.

14. The legend lives on from the Chippewa on down
    Of the big lake they call "Gitche Gumee."
    "Superior," they said, "never gives up her dead
    When the gales of November come early."

When the Saints Go Marching In

Words by Katherine E. Purvis
Music by James M. Black

Additional Lyrics

2. Oh, when the sun refuse to shine,
   Oh, when the sun refuse to shine,
   Oh, Lord, I want to be in that number,
   When the sun refuse to shine.

3. Oh, when the stars have disappeared,
   Oh, when the stars have disappeared,
   Oh, Lord, I want to be in that number,
   When the stars have disappeared.

3. Oh, when the day of judgment comes,
   Oh, when the day of judgment comes,
   Oh, Lord, I want to be in that number,
   When the day of judgment comes.

You Are My Sunshine

Words and Music by Jimmie Davis

1. The oth - er night, dear, _____ as I lay

(2., 3.) See additional lyrics

sleep - ing, _____ I dreamed I held you in my

arms. _____ When I a - woke, dear, _____ I was mis -

tak - en, _____ and I hung my

head and cried. _____ You are my sun - shine, _____

Additional Lyrics

2. I'll always love you and make you happy
   If you will only say the same.
   But if you leave me to love another,
   You'll regret it all someday.

3. You told me once, dear, you really loved me
   And no one else could come between.
   But now you've left me and love another;
   You have shattered all my dreams.

The Best Collections for Ukulele

The Best Songs Ever

70 songs have now been arranged for ukulele. Includes: Always • Bohemian Rhapsody • Memory • My Favorite Things • Over the Rainbow • Piano Man • What a Wonderful World • Yesterday • You Raise Me Up • and more.

00282413 . . . . $17.99

Campfire Songs for Ukulele

30 favorites to sing as you roast marshmallows and strum your uke around the campfire. Includes: God Bless the U.S.A. • Hallelujah • The House of the Rising Sun • I Walk the Line • Puff the Magic Dragon • Wagon Wheel • You Are My Sunshine • and more.

00129170 . . . . $14.99

The Daily Ukulele

arr. Liz and Jim Beloff
Strum a different song everyday with easy arrangements of 365 of your favorite songs in one big songbook! Includes favorites by the Beatles, Beach Boys, and Bob Dylan, folk songs, pop songs, kids' songs, Christmas carols, and Broadway and Hollywood tunes, all with a spiral binding for ease of use.

00240356 Original Edition $39.99
00240681 Leap Year Edition $39.99
00119270 Portable Edition $37.50

Disney Hits for Ukulele

Play 23 of your favorite Disney songs on your ukulele. Includes: The Bare Necessities • Cruella De Vil • Do You Want to Build a Snowman? • Kiss the Girl • Lava • Let It Go • Once upon a Dream • A Whole New World • and more.

00151250 . . . . $16.99

Also available:

00291547 **Disney Fun Songs for Ukulele** . . . $16.99
00701708 **Disney Songs for Ukulele** $14.99
00334696 **First 50 Disney Songs on Ukulele** . $16.99

First 50 Songs You Should Play on Ukulele

An amazing collec-tion of 50 accessible, must-know favorites: Edelweiss • Hey, Soul Sister • I Walk the Line • I'm Yours • Imagine • Over the Rainbow • Peaceful Easy Feeling • The Rainbow Connection • Riptide • more.

00149250 . . . . $16.99

Also available:

00292082 **First 50 Melodies on Ukulele** . . . $15.99
00289029 **First 50 Songs on Solo Ukulele** . . $15.99
00347437 **First 50 Songs to Strum on Uke** . $16.99

40 Most Streamed Songs for Ukulele

40 top hits that sound great on uke! Includes: Despacito • Feel It Still • Girls like You • Happier • Havana • High Hopes • The Middle • Perfect • 7 Rings • Shallow • Shape of You • Something Just like This • Stay • Sucker • Sunflower • Sweet but Psycho • Thank U, Next • There's Nothing Holdin' Me Back • Without Me • and more!

00298113 . . . . $17.99

The 4 Chord Songbook

With just 4 chords, you can play 50 hot songs on your ukulele! Songs include: Brown Eyed Girl • Do Wah Diddy Diddy • Hey Ya! • Ho Hey • Jessie's Girl • Let It Be • One Love • Stand by Me • Toes • With or Without You • and many more.

00142050 . . . . $16.99

Also available:

00141143 **The 3-Chord Songbook** $16.99

Pop Songs for Kids

30 easy pop favorites for kids to play on uke, including: Brave • Can't Stop the Feeling! • Feel It Still • Fight Song • Happy • Havana • House of Gold • How Far I'll Go • Let It Go • Remember Me (Ernesto de la Cruz) • Rewrite the Stars • Roar • Shake It Off • Story of My Life • What Makes You Beautiful • and more.

00284415 . . . . $16.99

Simple Songs for Ukulele

50 favorites for standard G-C-E-A ukulele tuning, including: All Along the Watchtower • Can't Help Falling in Love • Don't Worry, Be Happy • Ho Hey • I'm Yours • King of the Road • Sweet Home Alabama • You Are My Sunshine • and more.

00156815 . . . . $14.99

Also available:

00276644 **More Simple Songs for Ukulele** . $14.99

Top Hits of 2020

18 uke-friendly tunes of 2020 are featured in this collection of melody, lyric and chord arrangements in standard G-C-E-A tuning. Includes: Adore You (Harry Styles) • Before You Go (Lewis Capaldi) • Cardigan (Taylor Swift) • Daisies (Katy Perry) • I Dare You (Kelly Clarkson) • Level of Concern (twenty one pilots) • No Time to Die (Billie Eilish) • Rain on Me (Lady Gaga feat. Ariana Grande) • Say So (Doja Cat) • and more.

00355553 . . . . $14.99

Also available:

00302274 **Top Hits of 2019** $14.99

Ukulele: The Most Requested Songs

Strum & Sing Series
Cherry Lane Music
Nearly 50 favorites all expertly arranged for ukulele! Includes: Bubbly • Build Me Up, Buttercup • Cecilia • Georgia on My Mind • Kokomo • L-O-V-E • Your Body Is a Wonderland • and more.

02501453 . . . . $14.99

The Ultimate Ukulele Fake Book

Uke enthusiasts will love this giant, spiral-bound collection of over 400 songs for uke! Includes: Crazy • Dancing Queen • Downtown • Fields of Gold • Happy • Hey Jude • 7 Years • Summertime • Thinking Out Loud • Thriller • Wagon Wheel and more.

00175500 9" x 12" Edition $45.00
00319997 5.5" x 8.5" Edition $39.99

Order today from your favorite music retailer at
halleonard.com

Prices, contents and availability subject to change without notice

Disney characters and artwork TM & © 2021 Disney